The Faithful Father

Devotional Selections by Janette Oke

The Father of Love
Father of My Heart
The Father Who Calls

The
Faithful
Father
Janette Oke

Illustrations by Roselyn B. Danner

BETHANY HOUSE PUBLISHERS
MINNEAPOLIS, MINNESOTA 55438

Editorial development by Blue Water Ink,
Grand Rapids, Michigan

Artwork by Roselyn B. Danner

Published by Bethany House Publishers
A Ministry of Bethany Fellowship, Inc.
11300 Hampshire Avenue South, Minneapolis, MN 55438

Printed in the United States of America

Library of Congress Cataloging-in-Publication Data

Oke, Janette, 1935–
  The faithful father / Janette Oke.
      p.   cm.
    ISBN 1-55661-361-X :
    1. Meditations. I. Title.
  BV4832.2.04   1993
  242—dc20
                                                    93-27121
                                                    CIP

CONTENTS

Foreword	7
The Calling of Emily Evans	9
Julia's Last Hope	59
Roses for Mama	105
A Woman Named Damaris	155

FOREWORD

In the series *Women of the West*, we are introduced to a number of women all with different personalities and different situations. It is my hope as the writer that you, the reader, might be able to identify with one of the characters—be it Emily in her sincere dedication; Julia, who was willing to work to try to hold her family steady in a troubling time; Angela, who made a promise that she labored to keep; or Damaris, who nearly allowed her troubled past to keep her from a promising future, but who instead found faith, which enabled her to forgive and go on.

Your situation might not correspond with that of one of these characters, but I pray that their stories might nevertheless encourage you to live in quiet confidence and greater victory, knowing that God is always faithful concerning His promises.

JANETTE OKE

The Calling of Emily Evans

SURETY

Emily stood and bowed her head. Subconsciously her spirit began to quiet, her soul to respond. Fred Russell always seemed so close to God when he prayed. Emily wanted that more than anything in the world. She wished with all her heart that she knew his secret. She strained to hear every word of the prayer above the quiet rustle of the dining room. A new calmness descended upon her as she began to sense the presence of God.

When she sat down again at the table, a new attitude possessed her. Her tiredness and anxiety seemed to disappear. She knew without a doubt what she was doing here in school. She knew what she wanted with her own life. She knew that no matter how difficult it might be for her to keep up with the studies and the multitude of scheduling bells, she was where she belonged. Where she needed to be. She longed with every fiber of her being to know God better, to understand His way, to find His will for her scattery life. [20]

God doesn't play hide and seek with His will.
He reveals it to all who want to know it.

And this is life eternal, that they might know thee the only true God, and Jesus Christ, whom thou hast sent.

JOHN 17:3

SERENITY

It was all Emily could do to accomplish her assignments in time for the next day's classes. On more than one occasion she broke the lights-out rule, and she was occasionally late for breakfast—in spite of Ruth's insistence that she must get up. It seemed to Emily that she was always rushing, always pressing, always scurrying to keep up with the rest. Yet in all of the hurry, she was conscious of a strange serenity that she was in the right place, doing the right thing. Her knowledge of the Bible continued to grow daily.

To Emily the most special time of the day was chapel. She loved to hear the students singing hymns and giving testimonies, and she drank in the preaching. There was so much she longed to know. She felt unworthy to be at such a place of learning—yet deeply thankful that God had allowed her to come.

As far as Emily was concerned, Ruth was the perfect example of what a young Christian woman should be. Though rather plain in appearance, she was alert, capable, intelligent, and devout. Her no-nonsense approach to life fit well with her deep desire to serve the Lord. Emily thanked God many times for giving her a roommate like Ruth.

[29–30]

Don't expect peace from God
unless He can expect obedience from you.

Let no man despise thy youth; but be thou an example of the believers, in word, in conversation, in charity, in spirit, in faith, in purity.　　1 TIMOTHY 4:12

PREACHING

Mr. Evans was intrigued by the news that women were learning to preach. "Ordained?" he asked.

"No," Emily answered slowly, "Not ordained. But they preach—and they help in the church. And they lead people to the Lord too."

"Do they do everything a man preacher does?"

"No-o," Emily had to admit. "They can't do things like marry or bury. Or baptize. Things like that. But they preach. Mostly when their husbands have to be away. But some couples take turns."

"Well, I don't guess I'd care much to have a daughter of mine bein' a preacher—even if her husband was," went on Mr. Evans. "Seems to me that one preacher in a household is quite enough." He thought for a moment and then spoke again, quietly. "Not sure I'd want to be listenin' to a woman either, come to think of it."

"I think Ruth might like to be one," said Emily, speaking barely above a whisper. "She hasn't said so yet, but she loves to study and says that she would love to preach."

Emily's father was shaking his head. "Must be a strange one," he observed.   [33–34]

Everyone who follows God's call will be considered strange by some, but beautiful by God.

And how shall they preach, except they be sent? as it is written, How beautiful are the feet of them that preach the gospel of peace, and bring glad tidings of good things!

ROMANS 10:15

13

THE CALL

Scripture passages such as "Calling the twelve to him, he sent them out two by two" seemed to leap off the page and burn themselves into Emily's heart. What did it all mean? Emily did not wait patiently for the answer. She posed hard questions in class, sought counsel from fellow students, and listened intently in the worship services. Near the end of her first year of Bible school Emily received her answer.

"We have countless places where people are begging us to start a church, and we have no one to send," the chapel speaker was saying. "God does not call us to sit idly by while people perish. He has called us to go—to give—to preach the Gospel. We need to be willing to obey His voice as He speaks to us. Where are the men who are willing to bridge the gap—to answer, 'Here am I. Send me'? We, as a denomination, are here to send you forth. We are here to back and support you. We are here to help you to obey God's call—to take up your cross and follow Him."

Is he speaking only to the men? Emily wondered.

"If He is speaking to your heart, obey His voice—follow His leading today. Come. Acknowledge His call on your life. Come and kneel at the altar of prayer. Offer up your life as a sacrifice of love and obedience to the Lord who loves you."   [36–37]

Whom the Lord calls, He also empowers.

And he called *unto him* the twelve, and began to send them forth by two and two; and gave them power over unclean spirits.   MARK 6:7

SURRENDER

Unable to bear the intensity of feeling in her heart any longer, Emily rose hastily and practically ran to the altar railing where she knelt down and buried a tear-streaked face in her clasped hands.

The answer had come. If God had no helpmate with whom she could share His call, she would go alone. It was as simple as that. Will Pearson might think it impossible for a woman to preach, but Emily knew otherwise. Hadn't she heard God's call? Hadn't He promised all of His children that He would be with them? Of course! Of course God could call a woman to serve. Emily had no idea just where and how—but she did know that her heart yearned to be of service to God.

[37]

Those led by the power of God
cannot be stopped by the power of man.

Then Peter and the *other* apostles answered and said, We ought to obey God rather than men.

ACTS 5:29

15

CONVICTION

All that week Emily walked on air. She was actually going to serve God in a new work—somewhere. Even now she was preparing herself for that service. She would prepare herself well. She needed to thoroughly know the Word. She would be sharing it with hungry people Sunday after Sunday.

And then, unbidden, a new thought came to Emily. She remembered the late nights—the stolen minutes after lights out and the jumping into bed under false pretenses to fool the preceptress. Surely God could not honor such actions. She was smitten with conviction, and tears stung her eyes. She had to make things right before she could go one step further. She had to confess her sin and ask for forgiveness. *Maybe they will refuse me an assignment someplace when they know how deceitful I've been,* she thought, her heart constricting with fear.

[39]

Before we can move forward with God,
we have to clean up where we've been.

And they which heard *it,* being convicted by *their own* conscience, went out one by one, beginning at the eldest, *even* unto the last: and Jesus was left alone, and the woman standing in the midst.   JOHN 8:9

16

CONFESSION

The smile left Miss Herrington's face, but her eyes still held softness. "Go on with your confession," she urged.

"I—I haven't always been to bed on time. I—I mean I have studied after—after lights out. I—I need to spend much longer studying than Ruth, and so I—I—broke the rules."

"Do you understand why we have the lights out rule?"

"Yes." Emily's voice trembled. "So that we get the proper rest."

"Correct. You have been remarkably free of sickness this winter—but your faculty has been praying for you. Perhaps God has seen fit to answer those prayers in spite of your disobedience." Miss Herrington's gentle tone took some of the sting out of the words. "Because," she went on, "He saw a girl who wanted to get all she could from her studies. But, one should not be presumptuous with God. From now on I shall expect you to be in bed at the proper hour. If you need more study time, we will try to find some other way for you to manage it."

The woman's kindness surprised Emily. She had not expected such understanding. Yet strangely, she felt more chastised than if she had been scolded or assigned more kitchen duty. [40–42]

If your goal is to build up yourself, use harsh words;
if your goal is to build up others, use gentle ones.

Confess *your* faults one to another, and pray one for another, that ye may be healed. The effectual fervent prayer of a righteous man availeth much.

JAMES 5:16

17

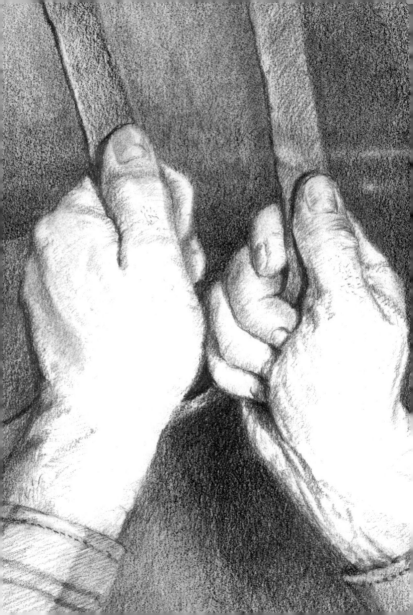

SACRIFICE

They were almost home before her father asked, "How's school?"

Emily's heart began to pound. *Is now the time to tell Father about my call?* She took a deep breath and decided to get it over with.

"We had a wonderful chapel service recently," Emily began. "Rev. Witt spoke about the need for church workers. Then he gave an altar call. He asked those who felt God was calling them to serve Him to step out and come forward. Eight students went forward."

Emily turned toward her father. His eyes were alight and he answered almost under his breath, "Praise God."

Emily knew her father was deeply interested in enlarging their mission of reaching local communities, particularly ones that had no church. Before the gleam could leave her father's eyes, Emily took another deep breath and blurted out, "I was one of them." She waited for the lecture to begin, but there was none. Only silence. His foot stirred restlessly on the wooden boards of the wagon and his hands tightened on the reins, but still he did not speak. He had just thanked God that young people had been called to preach. Now he had to face the giving of his own flesh and blood. [44–45]

*We cannot expect God to provide something
we are unwilling to give up.*

He that spared not his own Son, but delivered him up for us
all, how shall he not with him also freely give us all things?

ROMANS 8:32

SILENCE

They rode in silence. Emily could tell that her father was mulling over the news. Finally he spoke. "So who's the young man? When you were home at Christmas, you told about a preacher and his wife servin' together—"

"Oh," cut in Emily quickly, "I—I'm quite prepared to go alone."

"Alone?" he thundered. "That's absurd. You can't just go off and run a church alone. A young girl like you—sickly and—"

"I'm not sickly," Emily protested. "I've much more strength than you credit me with, Father. And I will have God to—"

"It's unheard of," her father continued, paying little attention to Emily's arguments. "It wouldn't even be decent for a young woman to be on her own. To try to manage a church. How can the district superintendent even consider such a thing? I won't hear of it! Not for one of my girls!"

Emily bit her tongue. Now was no time to continue the discussion. Tears stung her eyes, but she made no further comment. Instead she prayed that God would speak to her father. If she was to answer God's call, God would need to convince her father that it was proper and right for a young woman. [45–46]

There are times when God can speak more clearly through our silence than through our voices.

For I have not spoken of myself; but the Father which sent me, he gave me a commandment, what I should say, and what I should speak. JOHN 12:49

CONFIDENCE

The small community of Wesson Creek was Emily's first assignment. A small living accommodation was available, Emily was informed by the superintendent in his letter, so she would not be boarding. The town was a two-day drive from home by horse and buggy. Her father was providing her with a team of grays and a secondhand buggy.

Emily was relieved yet anxious about her assignment, for she had never lived alone. She would be glad for the solitude—it would help her in studying and prayer time—but at times it would be lonely too.

She felt thoroughly confused and strangely agitated as she watched her father reluctantly load the buggy, occasionally giving her long, questioning glances. She was both excited and fearful, exuberant and solemn, eager to be off and doubtful about leaving the home she had known and loved.

But she would not let the doubts and fears show. She kept the smile on her face, the spring in her step, and indicated that she was perfectly at ease with the path her life was taking. [53–54]

Even though we doubt our own abilities,
we can have confidence in God's.

Thou wilt shew me the path of life: in thy presence *is* fulness
of joy; at thy right hand *there are* pleasures for evermore.

PSALM 16:11

HUMILITY

As Emily approached the town she realized that her appearance was quite a mess. She had planned to put on her deaconess bonnet just before entering the town, but now she did not wish to disgrace the hat. She looked for an unobtrusive entry into the small town, but there seemed to be only one road leading into it—right down the main street.

Emily did not want to place the distinguishing bonnet upon her head. But she did. At the very edge of town, she brushed her hair back from her warm face and pushed stray brown curls into place before settling the bonnet on her head. She brushed the dust from her skirts and tried vainly to brush away the wrinkles as well, and then clucked again to her team.

If she was going to minister to these people, she had to be friendly, she decided. So with that determination, Emily headed into the heart of town, ready to greet anyone she met with a warm smile and a nod of her head.

Though it damaged her pride, she kept her resolve, smiling and nodding to all she passed as though she were properly groomed and attired.

[73]

If we're concerned about how we look to God, we'll have little concern about how we look to others.

Turn away mine eyes from beholding vanity; *and* quicken thou me in thy way.   PSALM 119:37

IMPERFECTION

When she reached a large building called Wesson Creek Mercantile, Emily pulled the horses up before the building next to it. According to her map, this was to be her home and the church for her parish.

It was not an impressive looking place. The paint had long since washed from the plain board sides. The door was sagging slightly, the two front windows dirty and broken, the walk in front of it covered with clutter. Emily looked at it in dismay. It couldn't be expected to draw people to worship.

For a moment she felt like crying, and then her sagging shoulders lifted and she forced a smile. It wasn't the building that mattered. She was here to share the Gospel. She would do that. [73–74]

God takes what is imperfect and
uses it for His perfect purposes.

But Christ being come an high priest of good things to come,
by a greater and more perfect tabernacle, not made with
hands, that is to say, not of this building.

HEBREWS 9:11

CHILDREN

Mrs. Travis turned to cut the bread and get the jam from her cupboard.

"So you're the new preacher?" Mrs. Travis said as she brought china cups from the cupboard. The cup that she handed Emily was without blemish, but the one she kept for herself had a large chip. She seated herself at the table and poured the tea.

"Well, I—I guess I don't really think of myself as a—a preacher," Emily fumbled. "More of a—a—teacher."

Mrs. Travis nodded. "Well, whatever you call it," she said, "we've sure been needing someone."

Emily's heart responded with a joyous flutter.

"I was raised in church myself," explained the woman, "but my babies—haven't had a bit of church—any one of them." Her eyes darkened. "Sometimes I fear that it's too late for some of them. They've already been shaped to be what they're gonna be."

"It's never too late for God," Emily said softly. [79]

*Children may learn about the Bible at church,
but they learn how to live it from their parents.*

Observe and hear all these words which I command thee,
that it may go well with thee, and with thy children after
thee for ever, when thou doest *that which is* good and right
in the sight of the Lord thy God.

DEUTERONOMY 12:28

DISCOURAGEMENT

Emily threw out the last of the dirty water, filled the basin with warm water, and thoroughly washed her hands, arms, and face. When she had finished, she turned to her kitchen supplies. She was much too weary to spend a lot of time cooking, so she reached for a frying pan, scrambled a couple of eggs, and sliced some of Ina's bread. Then she settled at the table and bowed her head in prayer.

She was thankful—truly thankful. But as she raised her head the room before her made her tired shoulders sag. *Will this ever look like a home?* Even with her scrubbing, she had succeeded only in uncovering more blemishes on the walls, more cracks in the windows, more worn spots on the painted floor boards.

The dirt was gone, but her unpacked boxes and bags were stacked all about. Would her things fit in this tiny place? What could she do for cupboard space? The one tiny cupboard would hold very little besides her few dishes. Emily sighed. It was going to be very difficult. [82–83]

A thorough cleaning always makes a bigger mess, but it's only temporary if we're persistent enough to finish the job.

Let integrity and uprightness preserve me; for I wait on thee.   PSALM 25:21

INDIGNATION

Emily wasn't sure which of them was more surprised at seeing the other. She scrambled to her feet, her eyes mirroring his surprise.

His smile, though slow in coming, was delightful. He nodded, then chuckled, "I'm not used to finding a girl in my woods."

"I'm not a girl. I'm Miss Emily Evans," she announced. Realizing that he still assumed her to be a young girl, she added, "I'm the new deaconess. The mission worker sent here to start a new church."

"Well, I expect you won't have much trouble finding a congregation," he teased. "A pretty young girl—I mean, woman. I guess your church knew well what it was doing."

"What do you mean?" Emily asked. "I have been sent here to start a mission, not to lure people to the church."

At the sound of his chuckle, she stopped. *He is insufferable!* she fumed. *I will not stay and have him mock me further.* With a defiant toss of her head she started back down the trail but was quickly jerked to a stop. Her hair had become entangled in a branch. [92–93]

When someone offends God, we have reason to be indignant;
when someone offends us, we don't.

And the ruler of the synagogue answered with indignation,
because that Jesus had healed on the sabbath day.

LUKE 13:14

TIMELESSNESS

While the men painted the walls, Emily scrubbed the wooden pews. Washing wouldn't cover the deep stains, but for now she would be content with having them clean. She was already getting more help than she had expected; she would not ask for more.

The men finished painting just before the supper hour and sat down for one last meal at Emily's table. Then the truck disappeared down the dust-covered street and Emily was left alone. Though dreadfully tired, she felt euphoric. It was only Thursday night. She had all day Friday and Saturday to make calls and invite people to the Sunday services. She could hardly wait to get started.

She lingered at the simple wooden pulpit trying to envision what it would be like to face her congregation on Sunday morning. Her finger idly traced a large gouge that traveled over the pulpit's entire surface. The scarred piece of furniture looked as if it had served for years in many missions.

But the battered pulpit could not daunt Emily's spirits. It was not the building or the furnishings that mattered. It was the Word. The Bible was pure and righteous and unscathed by time or wear or even indifference. She could hardly wait for the opportunity to share such good news with this little community. [97]

The old, old story is new every day.

For I am not ashamed of the gospel of Christ: for it is the power of God unto salvation to every one that believeth; to the Jew first, and also to the Greek.

ROMANS 1:16

FOOLISHNESS

With her Bible in one hand and the borrowed paint brush in the other, Emily set out. She would return the brush to the mercantile and begin her invitations there.

Emily entered the store and called merrily, "Good morning. I'm returning your brush. I can't thank you enough—"

"My what?" A gruff voice stopped her in her tracks.

"I—I'm sorry," Emily stammered, "I thought the owner was here."

"He is!" the man snorted.

Just then the woman who had helped Emily previously entered the shop. Relieved, Emily motioned in her direction, "I thought she—"

"Well, she don't," the man countered.

The woman, not a bit intimidated by the man's roar, approached Emily with an outstretched hand and accepted the brush.

"My brother owns the store," she explained. "I help out when he's not around." Then she added, "I see ya had some help with the church."

"Yes," Emily responded, her eyes shining. "It's ready now. I dropped by to extend an invitation for service. Ten o'clock."

"Reckon John and me don't feel much need for church," the woman answered firmly.

[98–99]

What people feel is not an accurate measure
of what they need.

For so is the will of God, that with well doing ye may put to silence the ignorance of foolish men.

1 PETER 2:15

29

FAITHFULNESS

Singing to herself, Emily prepared for the service. At two minutes to ten, Mrs. Travis and two of her children made their way into one of the pews. Emily smiled her good morning and waited another fifteen minutes, but no one else came. With a heavy heart, she started the Sunday school lesson. Maybe others would join them later for the morning service, but she was disappointed in that as well.

Don't despair, she told herself. *This is only the beginning. Perhaps God wants me to spend personal time with Mrs. Travis and her children.*

When the short Bible lesson and the worship service had ended, the woman took Emily's hand and smiled her appreciation. "It is good to be in church again," she said softly. "I have missed it so much. Especially since Mr. Travis is—is ill."

"I'm so glad you could come," Emily responded, giving the older woman a warm hug.

Emily lingered about the room, straightening the few worn hymnals and studying the stains on the walls. Her first Sunday had not been as she would have chosen. But certainly God cared even more about these people than she did. He would help her get their attention. [115–116]

Our job is to speak God's truth;
God's job is to get people's attention.

For the Son of man is come to seek and to save that which was lost.   LUKE 19:10

COMPARISONS

Emily's days were mostly taken up with her calling. At times she came home weary and disappointed. There just didn't seem to be much interest in her little mission church. With difficulty she left her burden with the Lord and tried to sleep in spite of her anxiety.

A letter from Ruth was filled with excitement and good news. She loved her community, she loved her boarding place, and she had crowded twenty-five people into one little country school-house on her first Sunday of preaching—twenty-nine in the other and the numbers had continued to grow. Now the attendance had settled in at thirty to forty at each service.

Ruth is such a good preacher that they are sure to come to hear her, thought Emily, holding the pages loosely and staring out at the vacant lot. She was happy for Ruth—but in comparison, Emily did seem to be a total failure. [118]

Comparing ourselves to others leads to reluctance;
comparing ourselves to God leads to reliance on Him.

For we dare not make ourselves of the number, or compare ourselves with some that commend themselves: but they measuring themselves by themselves, and comparing themselves among themselves, are not wise.

2 CORINTHIANS 10:12

31

PATIENCE

After tossing restlessly for some time, Emily crawled out of bed and knelt beside it. "Lord," she prayed, "I was sure I heard your call to serve, but maybe I misunderstood the feeling I had in chapel. I'm so mixed up. If you really want me to start this little church, then I need your help. I can't do it without you. Please, dear God—give me wisdom and direction. I'm willing to work here—for as long as it takes—if that is your will. Show me, Lord. Show me what to do. And help me to be patient. I know I'm always in a hurry. I know I push. I've always pushed myself, Lord. I'm not good at learning things and I've had to work harder at it than others. But help me to not push other people and to understand that this is your work, not mine. I don't need to push here. I need to obey. And I need to wait for you."

Emily continued praying, the tears wetting her cheeks. At length she felt a peace steal over her heart and she rose from her knees, brushed her tear-stained face with a sleeve of her nightgown, and climbed back into bed. She slept then. A restful, much-needed sleep. Whatever happened at Wesson Creek Mission was up to the Lord. Emily was only an instrument for Him to use. [118–119]

There is no need to hurry God;
He has all the time in the world.

Lead me in thy truth, and teach me: for thou *art* the God of my salvation; on thee do I wait all the day.

PSALM 25:5

RESPONSIBILITY

The next morning Emily arose in better spirits. It was Sunday and she planned to use the time with Mrs. Travis and her children as well as she could. But when the Travis children arrived, they were alone.

"Mama's not well," they informed Emily in quiet voices.

Emily was about to begin the lesson when the door opened again and Mrs. Reilly scurried in. She flashed a smile at Emily. "The cows got out. Just when we were ready to leave. George is still rounding up the last of them." She slid into the seat beside the Travis children. "Don't know why such things always happen on Sunday," she puffed.

Emily smiled and began her lesson. She had just announced the story of Noah and the ark when the door opened again and Sophie stuck her head in. "Sorry," she said. "They was scared to come alone the first time." She pushed four children with shiny-clean faces and slicked-down hair into the room, withdrew, and closed the door.

When it was time for the morning worship service, three more people joined them. *That's ten!* thought Emily, but she knew it was not her doing. God had sent them to her. Now it was her responsibility to teach from His Word. [119–120]

When God does what we ask,
we must be ready to do what He expects.

So then neither is he that planteth any thing, neither he that watereth; but God that giveth the increase.

1 CORINTHIANS 3:7

TURNING FROM GOD

Fallen leaves rustled beneath Emily's feet. Those that remained on the trees danced in the autumn breeze. In the sky, the Canada geese honked their goodbyes as they flew to warmer climates. Birds that would stay for the winter fluttered about to locate each berry tree and rose bush for future use. Squirrels scolded and bush rabbits ducked for cover when they saw Emily. She found great pleasure in the life of the woods, and she always found her way back to the same spot—the cluster of trees along the creek where she had met Shad Austin. Each visit to this restful hideaway refreshed Emily. On some days she brought her Bible and read as she basked in the serenity. Occasionally she wondered about the man she'd met there. Mrs. Reilly had not mentioned her nephew recently. Emily did not wish to pry, but she wondered why he had given up his calling and deserted his faith. What had happened to both of his parents? And when?

Her thoughts always led to prayer. She pictured the tears in Molly Reilly's eyes and heard again her words, "It would be an answer to his mother's prayers." So Emily added her prayers to those on Shad's behalf.   [127]

*Disappointment with God causes some people to turn their
backs on Him. Disappointment with us caused Him
to turn His face toward us.*

A wise son maketh a glad father: but a foolish son *is* the heaviness of his mother.

PROVERBS 10:1

34

ANGER

Emily greeted Big John graciously, but he only snorted in return.

"I—I need some soap," stated Emily, giving up on conversation.

"What kind?" he snapped. "Duz? Maple Leaf? Oxydol? Sunlight?"

"Which is the cheapest?" Emily asked.

"So ya bargain shop? Well, thet shows *some* sense."

"How big a box?" he asked. "Large or Family?"

"The smallest box—please," said Emily, her cheeks growing hot.

"Thought ya was bargain smart," huffed Big John. "Thet ain't wise buyin'."

"I would love to be a wise shopper, Mr. John," Emily said, her voice more stern than she intended, "but I only buy what I can afford to pay for." She dropped the money on his counter, spun on her heel, and left the store with the soap.

How that man riles me, she fumed and then felt guilty. She was to show love whether or not people were loving in return. She could never hope to win her neighbor if she responded that way. She turned and went back into the store.

"Ferget somethin'?" Big John gruffly greeted her.

"Y—yes," faltered Emily. "I—I forgot my manners and my Christian upbringing. I am sorry. Please forgive me." She turned and left the man staring after her, his mouth open in astonishment.   [130–131]

When anger gets the best of you,
it's time to make the best of anger: apologize.

Be not hasty in thy spirit to be angry: for anger resteth in the
bosom of fools.   ECCLESIASTES 7:9

35

DEPENDENCY

Everywhere Emily went people were talking about the fall picnic. Posters made by the school children began to turn up all over town. Word had it that Big John was going to provide some firecrackers for the event, and the farm kids were already coaxing their folks to stay late enough to watch them.

Emily wondered what she should bring as her share of the meal. Her grocery supplies were depleting rapidly, and she still faced the long winter months.

Maybe I should take a trip home and get some more, she thought, but it was such a long way to go and it was late enough in the fall that a winter storm could sweep in at any time. No, if she had been going to travel home for supplies, she should have done it weeks earlier.

She refused to write home to her father for money. She was sure he would send what he could if he knew of her plight, but she was on her own now—and serving the Lord. Didn't she believe that the Lord would provide? Where was her faith if she had to rush to her earthly father when the cupboard got a bit bare?

"Hold steady!" Emily often said to herself. "Be still, and know that I am God," she quoted from her beloved Bible.   [134–135]

> *One of the most difficult temptations to resist is the urge*
> *to depend on our own resourcefulness*
> *rather than on God's resources.*

Wait on the Lord: be of good courage, and he shall strengthen thine heart: wait, I say, on the Lord.

PSALM 27:14

NEGS

The attendance at the worship service was down. Emily was sure that many had found it difficult to get up after the previous day's celebrations. But George and Molly Reilly were there for Sunday school. Emily had wondered if Shad would accompany them and worried about how it might affect her presentation of the lesson if he did.

"Shad offered to do the chores to give George the morning off," Molly explained, and Emily felt both disappointed and relieved.

After the service Molly approached Emily. "I'm going to scoot on home and see to dinner," she said. "I'll send Shad in for you in half an hour or so."

Emily finished tidying the small church and then dumped the coins from the offering plate into the palm of her hand. She had been hoping for a bill or two—she was low on so many things she needed. Then she chided herself. She was not serving for the money. *I can't look to them for what I need any more than I can to my father,* she decided. "My God shall supply all your needs," she quoted aloud as she returned to her quarters to freshen up. [141–142]

Our needs are never greater than God's supply.

But my God shall supply all your need according to his riches in glory by Christ Jesus.

PHILIPPIANS 4:19

GOD'S GIFT

I could put on a new handle fer fifty cents," growled Big John.

Emily could hardly believe her ears. She'd been sure she would need to do the replacing herself, though she had no idea how.

"I—I'll take it," responded Emily as she counted out the coins.

"Why don't ya jest throw those coins in the offerin' on Sunday?"

Emily looked at the big man uncertainly. He stared back at her.

"Don't believe none in this here gospel stuff," he hastened to explain, "but always did like to carry a bit of insurance."

Emily slowly laid the change on the counter. "I'm afraid this Policy is all or nothing, Mr. John. It's not insurance—it's assurance." She held his eyes steadily.

Big John reached down, picked up the coins, and tossed them into his till. He said nothing more and neither did Emily.

"I'll have it ready fer ya to pick up in the mornin'," he finally said with a nod toward the shovel in his hands.

"Thank you," replied Emily softly. "I appreciate that," and she quietly left the store. [152]

God doesn't need the change we place in the offering,
but we need all the change He offers.

For by grace are ye saved through faith; and that not of yourselves: *it is* the gift of God.

EPHESIANS 2:8

PRAYER

Tears streamed down Emily's cheeks. She brushed at them with the back of her hand. *How can they live like this?*

Mrs. Travis was standing in the open doorway. Her dress was torn at the waistline and the skirt sagged sloppily into the snow on the doorstep. Her hair was dishevelled and Emily could see a small stream of blood coursing down her cheekbone. Mrs. Travis raised a shaky hand to wipe at it with the kitchen towel she held.

"Mrs. Travis," Emily called in a whispery voice as she led small Rena toward the woman. "May I help you? You could spend the night—" But the woman silenced her with a quick wave of her hand.

"We'll be all right now. He's sleepin'. He'll be okay in the mornin'." She reached out to pull her shaking daughter into her arms.

Emily hesitated. The woman needed to get back to her kitchen to tend to her own wounds. And Rena needed to be tucked close to the fire to chase the chill from her little bones.

Emily stepped back and turned to go. "I'll—I'll be praying for you," she whispered, but it seemed such a weak, empty promise to make under such circumstances. Emily drew a deep, shaky breath and turned away. [157]

When prayer seems like a small thing to do it is because we don't have God's big perspective.

In every thing by prayer and supplication with thanksgiving
let your requests be made known unto God.

PHILIPPIANS 4:6

UNPLEASANT TASKS

Mrs. Woodrow moved toward the back room. Soon she was back, a worn, threadbare black suit and a white shirt in her arms. "Here's his buryin' things," she said. "Guess he should be washed and shaved. There's water in the teakettle, and the basin is there on the corner stand. His razor's on that shelf."

She expects me to prepare the body for burial, thought Emily, the truth slowly sinking in. Woodenly, she moved toward the back room. It was cold, and a strange odor permeated it. Light from a small window outlined the still form on the bed. The man's eyes were fixed in a blank stare at the ceiling, and his mouth, empty of most of his teeth, hung open. Emily shuddered and wanted to run. She had never touched a dead body, let alone prepared one for burial. She had no idea what to do. "I can't do this," she whispered. "I can't." But then another thought flashed into her mind. *This might be the only bridge to reach the woman.*

"Dear God, help me," she prayed. "I need your help in a way I've never needed it before." Emily reached out a shaking hand to touch the man's arm. It was stiff and cold. Another shiver went through her, but she straightened her shoulders, pressed her lips tightly together, and began the unwanted task. [165–166]

Performing an unpleasant task may result in an opportunity to express unparalleled truth.

For though I be free from all *men,* yet have I made myself servant unto all, that I might gain the more.

1 CORINTHIANS 9:19

COMMITMENT

Emily wanted her hair and her dress to be just right for her evening out. She actually had a date with Ross, something she used to dream about. She smiled as she worked nervously at her hair.

Ross was prompt. He offered his arm and Emily took it shyly.

"You have a car?" she asked.

"Of course. I'm a man of great wealth now," he teased.

"Well, I'm not," admitted Emily. "I still use a poky old team and buggy. But then, an automobile would never make it through Wesson Creek's mud holes anyway."

"You really drive horses—through mud?" asked Ross.

"I do. Some of the women still have to walk when they make their calls. I am blessed with transportation—thanks to my father," admitted Emily.

"You shouldn't have to do that," Ross argued. "The men should be out there preaching."

"But there aren't enough men called," Emily countered. "Or, if they are—they aren't answering," she added slowly.   [176–177]

God can do more with a few people whose commitment is deep than with many whose commitment is shallow.

For ye see your calling, brethren, how that not many wise men after the flesh, not many mighty, not many noble, *are called*.   1 CORINTHIANS 1:26

GOD'S ANSWERS

How was yer trip?" Sophie asked.

"Great," answered Emily.

"Good," responded Sophie. "Things ain't been all thet great here. Nicky's been sick. I thought it was jest some little bug—but he didn't get no better, so I called Doc yesterday. He don't know what's the matter either." Tears started trickling down Sophie's cheeks.

Fear twisted a knot in Emily's stomach. "It isn't serious, is it?"

"Don't know. Doc don't even know what medicine to give."

"Oh, Sophie," said Emily softly, "we need to pray." She reached for Sophie's hand and bowed her head. "Dear God," she began, "we don't know what's wrong with Nicky, but you know all about him. Give the doctor wisdom as he seeks for the right medicine, and help Nicky to be better soon. And be with Sophie. It hurts to see a child ill, Lord. Help her to trust you and to be able to rest at night. Thank you, Lord, for all you do on our behalf. Amen."

"Thanks," muttered Sophie. "I was about beside myself with worry."

Emily gathered from Sophie's simple words that she considered her son as good as well. Emily felt a little fear. She had known the Lord long enough to realize that God's answers sometimes do not come quite as one asks. [180–181]

> *Prayer is not a way to get God to accept our will;*
>
> *it's a way to get us to accept His.*

O my Father, if it be possible, let this cup pass from me: nevertheless not as I will, but as thou *wilt*.

MATTHEW 26:39

Nicky died at quarter to three. There was nothing any of them could do to save him. Emily reached for Sophie to give all the support she could, but Sophie stepped back and pushed Emily's hands away.

"No!" she hissed. "Ya prayed. Ya asked God. Why did He let it happen? How could He? I was the one who was bad—not my Nicky." Sophie threw herself on the bed and gathered her son into her arms.

"Leave her," Dr. Andrew said softly to Emily. "She must express her grief in her own way. You go home now."

Emily left, dragging her tired body and her confused mind.

Over and over her own thoughts echoed those of Sophie. *Why? Why did it happen this way? Why didn't you heal him, Lord? You could have. You could have.*

Emily's faith had never been so shaken. *Will I ever be able to reach out to Sophie again? Will she ever let me?* She sobbed long into the night. When she finally did drift off she was totally spent emotionally.

[182]

*It's all right to ask God about His reasons
but not to reason that God was wrong.*

In thee, O LORD, do I put my trust: let me never be put to
confusion.   PSALM 71:1

43

REJECTING GOD

Emily visited Sophie three days after Nicky's death. Sophie greeted her cordially, but the coldness never left her eyes. Emily wished to offer some words of hope, but she didn't know how to express them. She prayed silently for wisdom—for guidance.

"I . . . I would love to have the children stay for dinner after church on Sunday," Emily began slowly.

"They won't be in church on Sunday," Sophie replied. "They'll not be goin' anymore."

"Oh, Sophie," breathed Emily before she could stop herself.

"Look, Emily," Sophie said frankly. "I don't mind callin' you a friend. Ya stayed with me and Nicky night an' day when he was sick, but don't ever try to shove yer religion at me again—understand? As I see it, either God couldn't do anythin' to save my son or He wouldn't. Either way, He's not the kinda God I want or need."

"Oh, He could have—" began Emily.

"Then why didn't He?" spat Sophie, her eyes flashing.

"I—I don't know," replied Emily. "I just don't know."

"Then don't be preachin' to me or to my children again!" [183]

The reason so few people find God is because they're looking for happiness rather than truth.

Strait *is* the gate, and narrow *is* the way, which leadeth unto life, and few there be that find it.

MATTHEW 7:14

44

REASONS FOR FAITH

Why are ya here?" Big John challenged. "No man ask ya to wed?"

Emily gulped down her frustration. If he only knew the agony she had been through trying to weigh her desires to be a wife and mother against her call to the ministry. She blinked back tears and answered softly, firmly. "Being here as a single woman is not easy. I do not enjoy trying to produce a garden in a patch of weeds. I do not like hauling wood and water. I do not even enjoy the preparation of sermons. But God has called me here. I do not know why—nor do I ask. I only try to obey." She picked up her small parcel. "And you can be assured," she went on, "I will be here just as long as I feel this is where He wants me." She turned and quietly left the store.

She was annoyed with herself that she let Big John's barbs get to her. She would never be any witness to the man as long as she allowed him to trouble her so.

"Lord," she prayed, "please help me to respond calmly to his honest questions and overlook the ones he asks simply to bother me. Help me to know what to say and how to say it. And help Big John to learn to love you." [196–197]

If we can't give a reason for our faith,
our faith is probably phoney.

But sanctify the Lord God in your hearts: and *be* ready always to *give* an answer to every man that asketh you a reason of the hope that is in you with meekness and fear.

1 PETER 3:15

A CHILD'S EYES

Emily got the fire going, placed the few hymnals on the seats, arranged her teaching notes on the small podium, and then waited. "There won't be many out this morning," she mused as she rubbed her hands together near the stove, trying to keep warm.

The door opened and Sophie pushed her head in. "May we come in?" she asked.

"Oh, Sophie!" Emily cried, hurrying to meet the woman.

Three beaming children bounded in ahead of their mother.

"We're comin' to church again!" exclaimed Olivia, clapping her small hands as she hopped across the floor.

"I'm so glad!" exclaimed Emily, and she knelt before the child and pulled her into her arms. "Oh, I have missed you," she said.

"We missed ya too," said Olivia, wrapping her arms around Emily's neck.

"It was the kids who made me see the truth," Sophie explained.

[199–200]

*Children give us a second chance to see God
through eyes undimmed by human understanding.*

A little child shall lead them.

ISAIAH 11:6

GOD'S WAYS

Sophie explained her change of heart. "Last night when I was puttin' the kids to bed, Tommie said, 'Mom, do ya think Nicky's in heaven?' And I said of course. Then he said, 'But if we don't live the way Jesus wants us to, we won't be able to go there to see him.' An' he started to cry. 'I want to see Nick again, Mom,' he said. And I knew I wanted to see Nick again too.

"But I didn't say so to Tommie. I jest couldn't let myself forgive God. An' then Johnnie spoke up. He said, 'Mom, do ya think that's why God let Nick die—so the rest of us would want to go to heaven?'" Sophie paused a moment to get control of her emotions.

"I couldn't answer thet question, but I thought about it long after the kids was asleep. Maybe that is why. I mean, if Nick had not died, I would've jest gone right on sendin' my kids to Sunday service, livin' my own life the way I want, never realizing thet I need God more'n any of 'em."

Sophie was crying hard now. Emily led her to a pew and they knelt together. Carefully, tenderly Emily led Sophie to understand and seek God's great forgiveness. [200]

God doesn't take anything
without giving something better in return.

The LORD gave, and the LORD hath taken away; blessed be the name of the LORD. JOB 1:21

EXPLAINING GOD

How can three people be one, answer me thet?" sneered Big John. "How can a person be spoken of as a son of God an' yet be God. How can ya be yer own son?"

"I don't know," Emily answered. "I don't think a human being can fully understand it. I don't think we have proper words to describe it. I think God called Christ His Son because that relationship was something we could understand. There are no words in our languages to describe the very special relationship of God the Father and God the Son."

"Pshaw!" exclaimed Big John. "Jest words to prove a belief ya can't support. When ya find reasons to believe all thet stuff ya teach—then maybe I'll listen to what ya got to say. Jesus was the Son of God—not God," the man insisted. "Don't tell me thet another man could do fer me what I ain't able to do fer myself!"

"I might not be able to explain it," Emily acknowledged, "but I believe it with my whole heart."

"Yeah, an' men used to believe the earth was flat."

Emily forced a smile and thanked him for her purchases as she left the store. There didn't seem to be any good reason to continue the argument. [202]

Trying to explain God in human language is like trying to build a skyscraper with a child's building blocks.

The Jews therefore strove among themselves, saying, How can this man give us *his* flesh to eat?

JOHN 6:52

48

HONEST DOUBT

During the weeks that followed, Emily spent hours studying her Bible, filling many pages with notes. *I must know for myself that Jesus is God,* she decided. *It is essential to my teaching—to my whole life. If it is not so—then my faith—my devotion—is all in vain.*

It was true, she discovered, that Scriptures referred to Him over and over again as the Son, and He himself made numerous references to the Father. *So they are two distinct beings,* Emily concluded.

Now Big John's next question haunted her. How could Jesus be the Son of God, and yet be God himself? Was He a created being, as some taught? Was He a lesser God, as others taught?

Emily struggled on. *What evidence do I have that Christ is God?* she asked herself as she dug more deeply into the pages of her Bible.

[203–204]

*Never discourage a sincere question—
honest doubt is better than dishonest faith.*

I and *my* Father are one.

JOHN 10:30

49

FAITH & DOUBT

As Emily dug more deeply into the scriptures, she began to discover some special evidence that Jesus was God. Christ forgave sins, something only God can do. And the creation passages refer to God and Christ as the Creator.

But it was the scriptures pertaining to the worship of God that caused Emily's heart to sing with joy. Scripture was very specific. God allows the worship of no being other than himself. He is a "jealous God." Man is to bow down to one God and one God only.

Yet God allows, yes, demands, the worship of His Son, Jesus Christ. In Philippians, Emily found the apostle Paul's statement: "At the name of Jesus every knee should bow, of things in heaven, and things in earth, and things under the earth; and that every tongue should confess that Jesus Christ is Lord, to the glory of God the Father."

"They have to be One!" cried Emily. "God would not share his honor with a lesser being. Christ was not just a son of God. He was God himself. One with the Father in purpose and being. [204–205]

Faith grows stronger when fertilized with doubt.

Wherefore God also hath highly exalted him, and given him a name which is above every name: That at the name of Jesus every knee should bow, of *things* in heaven, and *things* in earth, and *things* under the earth; And *that* every tongue should confess that Jesus Christ *is* Lord, to the glory of God the Father. PHILIPPIANS 2:9–11

GOD'S PROVISION

All Emily had left in her cupboard were a few cookies to serve to guests, a few teaspoonfuls of sugar, and enough tea for a skimpy pot. "Lord, I don't know what to do," she confided. "I can't beg. But I don't think you want me to starve. I hate to do it, Lord, but I guess I'll have to visit somebody. I—I determined that I would never do my calling just to get a meal—but this time . . ."

Emily decided to drive to the Reillys'. Not only would Mrs. Reilly feed her well, but she would send her home with more eggs and milk as well. That would keep Emily going for several more days. She pulled on her heavy coat and tied a warm scarf snugly about her neck. Then she took a deep breath and pushed against the door. The frost had sealed the edges. Emily pushed harder and felt it give. Her breath preceded her in silvery puffs. "It's too cold for man or beast," she said aloud, closing the door tightly behind her.

As Emily turned to go, her foot kicked against something. A small basket wrapped in brown paper lay at her feet. Emily picked up the basket, returned to the kitchen, and tore open the package.

"It's food!" she exclaimed, unable to believe her eyes. "It's food." Inside was a small bag of sugar, another of flour, and some vegetables, cheese, and bread. [205–206]

> *God's supply is more than adequate; it's our inadequate system of distribution that causes some people to go hungry.*

For the scripture saith, Thou shalt not muzzle the ox that treadeth out the corn. And, the labourer *is* worthy of his reward. 1 TIMOTHY 5:18

LEANING ON GOD

All through the long winter, Emily continued to get weekly supplies. None of her congregation knew anything about the source of the baskets. Emily thought they might be coming from Sophie, though Sophie was hard pressed to care for her own family's needs. The Reillys were not bringing it. They would have brought it openly had they known Emily was in such need, Mrs. Reilly told her.

Others too were surprised that Emily had been so low on provisions.

"But the cookies?" asked Mrs. Cummings. "You always had store-bought cookies."

"That was all I could afford," admitted Emily. "I didn't have enough money to purchase all the ingredients at any one time."

"Oh, my," said Mrs. Reilly sorrowfully, "if only we'd known. I can't forgive myself for allowing you to go hungry."

But Emily only smiled. "Don't feel guilty," she assured them all. "God meant it for good. I learned more about leaning on the Lord this winter than I have in my whole life. I learned the wonderful truth about faith and trusting God." [207]

*Only when our own resources are lean
do we truly learn to lean on God.*

I know both how to be abased, and I know how to abound:
every where and in all things I am instructed both to be full
and to be hungry, both to abound and to suffer need.

PHILIPPIANS 4:12

LOVING TOO MUCH

When Emily was sure the children were sleeping, she fixed another cup of tea for Mrs. Travis. Mr. Travis was quiet now, but Emily felt anxious and uncomfortable. Would they just sit and watch him die? "Shouldn't I get Dr. Andrew?" she asked.

"He's been," said the woman. "Nothing he can do. It's just a matter of time." She reached out and took the fragile hand of the man on the bed and stroked it gently—lovingly. "Suppose you wonder how I can still love him. Well, I haven't always loved him. Sometimes I hated him—with such a passion that I could have killed him—because of the way he was hurting the children. But one day I was reading my Bible, trying to find some sense to life, when I came across a verse that says we're forgiven just as much we forgive. Well, that stopped me right there. I knew that if I was ever to have peace with God, I had to forgive him. At first I thought I'd never be able to do it. And I couldn't have—in my own strength. But God helped me. I did forgive—and with that forgiveness I learned to love again. Oh, not like at first. Not like I loved the young man who won my heart long ago, but rather like a mother. He was not just hurting us—but himself. I sometimes think that he has suffered most of all. And so, though I could no longer respect him, I didn't hate him either. I loved—but in a different way." [212–213]

The idea that we can love too much
does not come from God.

Lazarus is dead. . . . Jesus wept. Then said the Jews, Behold
how he loved him! JOHN 11:14, 35–36

LAST CHANCE

He'll not make it this time," Mrs. Travis said quietly, "an' it grieves my heart for I know he isn't ready to go. He hasn't prepared to meet his Maker. There isn't one thing more I can do to help him. He's made his own choices—and he must face the consequences. I have prayed over and over that he be given one more chance to start over. And God has answered that prayer—time and again. Now I realize that he will not change. No matter how many chances he is given, he will always choose whiskey over God."

Emily left the room to tend the fire. "God," she prayed, "I've asked often for this family to be relieved of their suffering and pain—but I didn't mean this way, Lord. Isn't there another way? Is she right? Has he had his last chance?"

All through the long night and into the next day they kept their vigil. At two o'clock he breathed one last struggling breath and lay still. "It's over," Mrs. Travis said sorrowfully. "You can send for Doc Andrew now. He will need to prepare a death certificate."

Emily nodded and left for town. "Oh, God," she prayed, "if he only had made his peace with you. I had so hoped and prayed . . ." But Emily had to face the truth that there would be no more chances for Wilbur Travis.   [213–214]

One wrong choice may prevent us from making many right ones. Or vice versa.

Wine is a mocker, strong drink is raging: and whosoever is deceived thereby is not wise.

PROVERBS 20:1

S had ran a hand through his thick hair and laughed nervously. "Well, I guess the best place to start is at the beginning." He laughed again and reached for Emily's hand. "Remember when we first met?" he asked.

Emily nodded slowly. She didn't suppose she would ever forget.

"Well, you—you impressed me. The way you took my teasing. Your seriousness over your call to the ministry. But at the same time—to think of you as the preacher in town made me—well, I felt mixed-up and angry. You see, my father had been a preacher—and at one time I thought that I would be a preacher too. Then my mother got sick. Really sick—but there was no money for a doctor. We watched her get weaker and weaker every day. And then, without warning, we lost Dad. He had been the strong one—but suddenly he was gone—a heart attack. There was no money, no pension, no place for us to live. We had to move into a tiny two-room shack, and I watched as Mother's health continued to fail. I decided then if that was the way God took care of His preachers, I wasn't going to be one. And I told Mother so in no uncertain words." [218–219]

> *When it seems as if God has turned His back,*
> *perhaps it's because He's leading us in a new direction.*

For the gifts and calling of God *are* without repentance. For as ye in times past have not believed God, yet have now obtained mercy through their unbelief.

ROMANS 11:29–30

FAITHFULNESS

Uncle George and Aunt Moll came and got us," explained Shad. "And we lived with them until Mother's death. As soon as Mother was gone, I headed for the city and a job that would care for me in my old age. I had a good job—when I met you. But I wasn't happy. And there you were, a little bit of a girl, struggling with the work of running a church. I knew that if I—and other young men like me—hadn't shirked my responsibilities, you wouldn't need to carry all that weight alone. It bothered me. But I tried not to let it show. Instead, I had the crazy idea of wooing you away from your calling." He smiled softly at Emily. "Well, that didn't work either. You put me in my place, in quick order. And I also realized that if it had worked, I would have been terribly disappointed in you. I guess I wanted you to be stronger—more committed—than I had been. But I still couldn't get away from the fact that you had been true to your calling and I had turned my back on it. It bothered me—day and night."

[219]

Faithfulness is contagious.

Moreover it is required in stewards, that a man be found faithful.   1 CORINTHIANS 4:2

MOTIVES

At last I decided to do something about it. I wasn't happy anyway. I might as well do what I had been called to do. So I made things right with the Lord and set off to do what I should have done in the first place. I quit my job and went off to train for the ministry."

Emily's eyes grew big. "You're a minister?"

"Not quite. I still have some more schooling ahead." His grip on her hand tightened.

"What will Aunt Moll say?"

Shad laughed. "Aunt Moll has already said everything there is to be said."

"She knows? She never said a thing to me."

"That's because I asked her not to. I wanted to be sure," he explained. "Sure that I was going into the ministry for the right reasons. Because I had a call—not because I had a crush." [220]

To please others is a good motivation.
To please God is the best motivation.

And they went forth, and preached every where, the Lord working with *them*, and confirming the word with signs following.   MARK 16:20

57

ANSWERED PRAYER

I care for you, Emily. Deeply. You have both my respect and my love. I was hoping—praying—that you might honor me with permission to call—to write when I'm away—and perhaps, if God wills it . . ."

Emily's breath caught in her throat. Was she hearing him correctly? She wanted to answer but she couldn't find the words.

"I know this is sudden—that I have no reason to think you care at all for me—except the look in your eyes long ago when you told me that you'd pray. Have you prayed, Emily?" Shad looked searchingly into Emily's eyes. "And your answer?"

Emily swallowed. "It—it would seem the answer is yes," she whispered. "God has called you, and you are choosing obedience. I—I have never had a prayer answered more fully."

Shad smiled and pulled her into his arms. "I'm so glad God answers prayer," he whispered.

Emily blushed. "Oh, but I didn't pray for this," she protested, drawing back, her face red at the thought that Shad might think she'd prayed for his love.

But Shad quickly silenced her. "I did," he said softly as his arms closed about her, holding her tenderly, his cheek against hers. "I did. If God so willed." [221–222]

*It is not wrong to pray for what we want
unless we want something that is wrong.*

What shall we then say to these things? If God *be* for us, who *can be* against us? ROMANS 8:31

58

Julia's Last Hope

BLESSING

Julia Harrigan was in the east parlor, her back turned to the warm rays of the Saturday morning sun. She hummed softly as her hands worked a dainty hem in a new tablecloth, and she smiled as the smooth English linen slipped through her fingers. She did love fine things. From the dining room came the contented sound of Hettie's low, rich singing as she cleared away the remains of the morning breakfast.

A gentle squeaking sound coming from the porch told Julia that her two daughters were seated in the double porch swing. She imagined their yellow-gold hair reflecting the morning sun, their wide, frilly skirts fanned out across the whiteness of the painted seat. Then the swing became silent, and Julia heard footsteps cross the veranda as the girls moved on to some other activity, chattering as they went.

Again Julia smiled. Life was good. God had certainly blessed them.

[11]

With great blessing comes great responsibility.

Every man also to whom God hath given riches and wealth, and hath given him power to eat thereof, and to take his portion, and to rejoice in his labour; this *is* the gift of God.

ECCLESIASTES 5:19

61

CHOOSING LOVE

Everything about the house spoke of quietness and calm. Julia had always dreamed of having a home that would convey to her family and guests strong feelings of tranquility. Knowing this, John gave her every opportunity to create a peaceful atmosphere in their home.

Raised in the East and educated in a fine school, Julia had been brought up to be a woman of gentle spirit. But when she met the young John Harrigan, a rugged westerner, she did not hesitate to make her choice known. Even her father was amazed at the way she put her dainty foot down.

"I want to marry him," she insisted.

"Think, girl!" her father roared. "You are used to finery and ease. Do you think this woodsman will be able to provide it for you?"

"I really don't care," she responded. "Surely there is more to life than tea parties and silk dresses."

"Yes, there is more to life. There is poverty and need and hungry, unkempt children. But I do not wish it for an offspring of mine."

She pleaded then. "Oh, Papa. Please—I beg of you, don't send him away. I would rather have little with this man by my side than a fine mansion and someone I don't love." [12]

To love and be loved is the greatest of all God's gifts.

Better *is* a dinner of herbs where love is, than a stalled ox
and hatred therewith.

PROVERBS 15:17

THE NATURE OF LOVE

Life took an unexpected turn when John's uncle came to them in need. Born and raised in the wilds, Uncle George was a salty, rough man, and Julia felt uneasy around him. But he was John's kin, and when he took ill, Julia suggested he move into their spare room.

By the time he died, Julia had changed her mind about Uncle George. She had learned to love him in the time that she had waited on him. "I will miss him," Julia said softly. "He really had a special sweetness about him."

"I never thought I'd hear you call Uncle George sweet," John teased. "Remember how uncomfortable his quick, sharp tongue used to make you? But Uncle George surprised us, didn't he? Underneath all that, he had a sweet spirit. We both will miss him."

And then the unexpected. Stashed away in a local bank was a large sum of money from a gold strike. No one knew about it until after Uncle George's death, when John and Julia learned that he had left it all to them "as thanks for all you have done in caring for and loving a grouchy old man."

[13–14]

Acts of kindness precede feelings of love.

And beside this, giving all diligence, add . . . to godliness brotherly kindness; and to brotherly kindness charity.

2 PETER 1:5, 7

IMPRESSIONS

There wasn't much entertainment in town, but Julia had never needed outside excitement or activity to make her happy. Julia and John were heavily involved in their church, and that, plus a few community and social events, was enough for both of them.

Julia held a simple but deep faith. Never had John met anyone with the strong personal commitment to God that Julia possessed. She was like a child in her trust of the Savior.

The community developed a proprietary attitude toward the Harrigans, as though the family in the fine house belonged to the town. Their gentility added refinement to the whole settlement. "The Harrigans live just over yonder," folks would boast to any newcomer who would listen. "Hardly a stone's throw from our door. Such a fine family, the Harrigans. Such a proper lady she is—but totally without airs. Greets you on the street like any ordinary soul. Even has ladies in for tea. Fine folk."

Some may have envied Julia Harrigan her fine lace curtains and thick rich carpets, but there was no malice toward her. Julia did not flaunt her finery, and no one ever accused her of snobbery. [15]

People are impressed by wealth;
God is impressed by righteousness.

Thus saith the Lord, Let . . . not the rich *man* glory in his riches: But let him that glorieth glory in this, that he understandeth and knoweth me.

JEREMIAH 9:23–24

GOD'S PROVISION

John looked directly into Julia's eyes. "You must be in shock, just as I was. You still don't understand."

"I am not in shock. I am in my right mind. The mill will close. That means you will be without a job. But you can get another job. You have fine references. If there is no job in lumber—you can learn something else. You have a good mind—and a strong back. There will be other jobs—somewhere."

"Yes," he admitted, "If it wasn't for the house."

"We can sell the house and buy another," offered Julia. She hoped John had not read the agony in her eyes. She loved their house.

He shook his head slowly. "Without the mill, the town will die. There will be no sale for the houses, any of them. The property will be worthless—useless. It will become a ghost town."

His words made Julia's breath catch in her throat. Her hand trembled slightly against his sleeve. But then she lifted her chin and willed determination to return to her eyes. "God has always provided for us," she declared fervently. "He will not forsake us now—when we need Him the most."   [25–26]

When circumstances threaten to take what we have,
we have more room for God to give us what we need.

For the Lord loveth judgment, and forsaketh not his saints;
they are preserved for ever.

PSALM 37:28

CHANGE

Neither John nor Julia saw the twins standing in the doorway. And neither heard them as they left for their own room.

Jennifer broke the silence. Her face was ashen, her eyes filled with fear. "What will we do?" she whispered hoarsely.

Felicity had thrown herself on her bed and was sobbing.

Jennifer placed a protective arm around her sister's shaking shoulders and stroked her long blond hair. "You heard Mama—God will show us what to do. He knows all about the mill. Perhaps Papa will find another job—"

Jennifer walked to the window. Her eyes scanned the street, the neighboring houses, the small town with its church spire and school yard, the mountainside that rose in the distance. She loved it here. She would hate it if they had to leave. Why couldn't things continue as they always had? Surely there was some way—Jennifer squared her shoulders and turned to Felicity. "If we have to go—we must make it as easy for Mama and Papa as possible. You can take your treasures with you," she said, trying to console her sister.

"But I—I can't take my friends or—"

"We'll be all right," Jennifer assured Felicity again, wishing with all her heart that she felt as confident as her words sounded. [27–28]

> *If nothing ever changed we wouldn't have to fear that life*
> *would get worse, but we couldn't have hope*
> *that it would get better.*

For thou *art* my hope, O LORD God: *thou art* my trust from my youth.   PSALM 71:5

CONFIDENCE

After dinner, John lifted the family Bible from the bureau and turned the pages absentmindedly. He knew he had to tell the girls about the mill, but he wasn't quite sure how to do it, what to say. True, changes were in store for all of them—but what changes?

He knew Julia was right. Of course God would care for them—just as He had always done. But God had assigned the care of the family to the father of the home, and John felt as if he were failing his family. Even though he was not responsible for the closing of the mill, he still felt the guilt. He wanted to supply for the needs of his family as he had done in the past.

Though he tried to appear confident, his shoulders sagged. He had spent the afternoon with other men from the lumber mill, and the conversation always came back to the same stark truth. There would be no work in this small town once the mill closed. And there would be no sale for property—no matter how fine it might be. The little town of Calder Springs would soon be a ghost town.

Julia reached for John's hand and tried to encourage him with one of her confident smiles—though deep within her heart she felt little confidence.

[34–35]

Confidence comes only from God,
but comfort we can give each other.

Wherefore comfort yourselves together, and edify one another, even as also ye do.

1 THESSALONIANS 5:11

TREASURES

Jennifer took charge. She moved everything from the closet floor and placed it in a heaping pile before her sister. "Here," she said. "Sort it out. Make a pile of the things that aren't worth saving. I'll hang your clothes properly."

Felicity didn't argue. She dropped to the floor and began to rummage through her possessions. She gazed at the dried wild flowers, still stuffed in a glass vase long since void of water. How could she throw away things that represented a part of her life? Sighing, Felicity scooped up her treasures, knowing she would be unable to discard any of them. "What we need is separate rooms," she announced. "There isn't enough room in this dinky closet."

"It's the same size as mine," Jennifer reminded her twin.

"Yes—but you—" Felicity stopped. How could she express the fact that Jennifer didn't have treasures without sounding harsh? "You—you don't have—have as many things to put away."

"That's because I throw out the junk," Jennifer stated.   [22–23]

If we fill our homes with earthly treasures
we won't feel at home in heaven.

Lay not up for yourselves treasures upon earth, . . . For where your treasure is, there will your heart be also.

MATTHEW 6:19, 21

69

FAITH

Do you think Mama's plan could work?" Jennifer asked Hettie.

"Why not?" responded the older woman. "Your mama is a capable woman. When she puts her mind to something, it is likely to happen."

"But people around town are saying it's a crazy idea—just a silly dream," Felicity dared to state.

"An' who's sayin' that?" asked Hettie, her eyes flashing.

Felicity shrugged. "I don't know. I just heard—"

"Well, you don't listen none to such talk. You hear? Folks should at least give your mama a chance to prove herself." Hettie sighed as she lifted a pan of corn bread from the oven. "Your mama has been doing all she can. She has sent off a number of letters to see what kind of interest there might be in a tourist town here. We have about as nice a location as one could want. Beautiful mountains, pretty lakes, nice fishing streams. Your mama has summed it all up in her letters."

"But some of our friends have left already."

"Some folks don't have much faith," said Hettie.

Jennifer lowered her head. She wasn't sure just how strong her own faith was, but she wouldn't admit as much to Hettie. [43–44]

When in faith we lift a foot to follow God, God in
faithfulness sees that we put it down in the proper place.

A man's heart deviseth his way: but the LORD directeth his
steps.   PROVERBS 16:9

70

HOUSES & HOMES

Hettie placed the pot on the kitchen table and took the chair opposite Julia. "You're still worryin'?" she asked.

"Well, I try not to—but—frankly—I have no idea if anyone will ever want to come to our little town for a vacation. If it doesn't work—I've got these poor women believing in a dream that can never be. It would be better if—"

"Now you stop your fussin'. At least you're tryin'. No one will fault you if it doesn't work out."

"I've prayed and prayed," continued Julia, "and I'm still not sure I'm doing the right thing."

"Well, if it isn't, you can still do as the others. Quit and move." Hettie made the comment with a bit of contempt for those who had so easily given up.

"Oh, Hettie—I—I would be glad to go if—if only it wouldn't be so hard on John. Do you know the first thing that came to his mind when he told me the news?" Julia asked. "The house. Leaving the house. I hadn't known how important it was to him until then. If it wasn't for that—I'd move tomorrow. There are other houses. I love this house too—but for me it—it isn't the house that brings happiness. It's the ones you share it with." [46–47]

A house provides a shelter for the body;
a home provides shelter for the soul.

I will appoint a place for my people Israel, and will plant them, that they may dwell in a place of their own . . .

2 SAMUEL 7:10

ENJOYING WEALTH

I've always lived in a big house. Bigger and more elegant than this one. We rattled around in it. After Mama died there was just Papa and me and the servants—and Papa was rarely home. Do you know what, Hettie? I used to love walking along streets where the houses were small and crowded together and children played in tiny yards and mothers leaned over fences to chat with one another. I listened to the laughter and the chatter—and even the childish squabbles—and I envied those people until I was ashamed of myself."

Julia stopped to stir sugar into her tea, tears forming in the corners of her eyes.

"It wasn't that I didn't enjoy all the nice things in our big house," she went on. "It's just that it—it wasn't as important as having a family to love. But Papa—Papa always felt that fine things were so important—and he taught me to appreciate nice things too. But if I have to do without one or the other—things or family—things don't seem very significant." [47]

It is better to have a small house filled with love
than a big house filled with loneliness.

A man to whom God hath given riches, wealth, and honour,
so that he wanteth nothing for his soul of all that he desireth,
yet God giveth him not power to eat thereof, but a stranger
eateth it: this *is* vanity, and it *is* an evil disease.

ECCLESIASTES 6:2

John never had a big house—or nice things. His folks pioneered on the prairie. He spent his first years in a sod shanty. He was twelve years old before they even had a wood floor. His mother had to carry water from the stream and carry chips for her fire. She did her laundry in a big tub—on a metal scrubboard. Even after they moved into the wood house—with real glass panes in the windows—she still had none of the things that make life easier."

"Many women did that," recalled Hettie, thinking of her own mother.

Julia sipped the sweet tea from her china cup.

"For our first few years—I did it too," admitted Julia. "It really wasn't so bad. A lot of work—but I had the time to do it. It's funny, I have never felt as loved and cared for as I did in those first few years. I—I don't mean that I don't feel loved now," she explained quickly. "John still looks after me in every way—but we shared and planned in a different way then. We only had each other. We didn't have you for the kitchen—or your Tom for the gardens—or Rose to help with the cleaning and serving. I guess there is a different feeling when you do the caring for each other—with your own hands."

[47–48]

Only when we give of ourselves
do we give a gift of any value.

By love serve one another.
GALATIANS 5:13

I f my girls don't have all the nice things—if they have to rough it just a bit with the man each chooses to marry, I won't feel sorry for them. If they really love each other—if they work together to make a home—even a small, simple place that is their own little haven— if they care enough to seek the happiness of each other—then I will consider them blessed.

"I have been blessed—more than I realized," Julia continued. "I have had both. A lovely home and a loving family. Maybe I have had more than my share. Maybe I haven't had the sense to be as thankful as I should have been. God forgive me if I have taken it all for granted."

Hettie was about to defend her young mistress again, but Julia kept talking.

"Well, no more. I have sorted out many things in the last few weeks. This I know. God is still in charge of my life. He knows what I need and what is just pleasant baggage. If I must forfeit the baggage—I will not pout. But since it is important to John, I will do my best to hold things together—for him—and for the girls."

[48–49]

Losing earthly possessions helps us see more clearly the value of spiritual ones.

Your Father knoweth what things ye have need of, before ye ask him.   MATTHEW 6:8

HARDSHIP

John drew his final wage and headed home. He had decisions to make. Difficult decisions. He had been holding them at bay, but he could delay them no longer. He had to face reality and find a way to provide for his family. He was proud of Julia. She had rallied the town women, determined to fight to save her beautiful house on the mountainside. The house meant a lot to Julia, John reasoned. But he had the sickening feeling that no matter how hard she tried, she would end up brokenhearted. There was no way enough people would be drawn to Calder Springs. Already Banff was becoming a tourist attraction. And farther up the Rocky Mountain chain was Jasper. It too was growing in popularity. There were only so many people with money to spend at resorts.

John sighed deeply. It was hard for him to see Julia lose what she loved so much. It was hard to face the fact that the girls—who had been born to plenty—might now have to do without. He knew all about hardship. He could live simply. But his family? Except for the first few years of their marriage, John and Julia had lived well. And the girls had never known hardship. [54–55]

Hard times make strong people.

Who shall separate us from the love of Christ? *shall* tribulation, or distress, or persecution, or famine, or nakedness, or peril, or sword?

ROMANS 8:35

SUFFERING LOSS

John recalled his secret dream of one day owning a business of his own. He had never told anyone. Not even Julia, for he deemed the dream impossible—selfish. Uncle George's money had been a temptation—but only for a brief moment. He would not have considered using it to fulfill his own ambition. Julia's house was always uppermost in his mind.

Still, on occasion, he thought about that little business. A woodshop. A place where he could take the rough wood that came from the forest and shape and polish it until it shone like glistening dark gold beneath his fingers. He loved the touch of wood—the smell—the pattern of its grain.

If they could have sold the big house—even for a fraction of what it was worth—they might have had a possibility of starting over. As it was, they would lose the house, lose everything. John's jaw twitched and his eyes hardened. It would be tough giving it all up. He tried to shrug off his dismal mood.

"As Jule says," he reminded himself, "God didn't pack up and move off with the mill. He's still here—still looking after us."

[55–56]

Life's greatest gains often begin
with life's most alarming losses.

He that loseth his life for my sake shall find it.

MATTHEW 10:39

HARD WORK

Spring passed into summer. The eight women on Julia's committee continued their industrious labors. Each week they placed more items on the shelves in their little craft store. Julia laid aside her plans to use the new linen tablecloth herself. Instead, she pinned a price tag in one corner of it and placed it on the merchandise shelf.

Soon they would be receiving requests for accommodation in their new resort town. Those who had extra bedrooms had them ready and waiting—with outdoor-fresh linens on cozy beds, newest towels hanging on door racks, and shining windowpanes behind freshly laundered curtains.

But with every mail delivery, letters requesting accommodation were conspicuously absent. In spite of brave smiles and determined brightness, morale began to sag. They tried not to let it show—but it was there, dogging their footsteps, causing them to add more water to the soup pot, less meat to the stew.

For Julia it meant more feverish involvement. Her efforts increased. More letters written. More doilies crocheted. More hours spent coaxing and caring for her garden. [63]

Easy Street isn't found on God's road map.

And the LORD God took the man, and put him into the garden of Eden to dress it and to keep it.

GENESIS 2:15

CERTAINTY

John was torn. He wanted Julia to keep their lovely house. He wanted her venture to succeed, the town to be revived, but he had to admit that things looked grim. Funds were very low. If it weren't for Julia's big garden—if Tom and Hettie hadn't agreed to work for room and board—if Rose hadn't moved away with her family, if they didn't get free firewood from the old mill site—if—

But John tried to be positive. The first guests were soon to arrive, and Julia was sure that many more would follow. She was even concerned about where they would house them all once they started coming. With the shops opened and their shelves filled with baked goods, wild jams and jellies, handcrafted doilies, quilts and aprons, she was sure folks would enjoy strolling down Main Street.

To help Julia keep her dream alive, John kept the town looking as neat as he could. Snip, snip, went his clippers. From vacated yard to vacated yard, he snipped. *What if the venture didn't work? How long could he let Jule pursue her dream before he stepped in? Would it crush her?* Snip. *He could never build her another house like the one they had now. Should he suggest sending her and the girls back east to her father while he tried to get established again?* The thought made John cringe. "If only I knew what to do," he sighed. "If only I could be sure." [70–71]

> *When we are uncertain as to the right thing to do,*
> *we can be certain of the right reason for doing things.*

Whatsoever ye do, do all to the glory of God.

1 CORINTHIANS 10:31

DOING OUR BEST

"Mama," Felicity exploded, "that boy is trying to tip over the swing! He said he's going to go so high that it flips right over."

"Oh my!" exclaimed Julia on her way to the back porch.

Tom was there by the time Julia arrived. He couldn't reason with the young boy, and he couldn't discipline the guests' child, but he could thwart his action. Tom's big, broad hand held the swing firmly so the boy, push as he might, went nowhere.

Julia thanked Tom and returned to the kitchen. Felicity and Jennifer followed her.

"How long will he be here, Mama?"

"He kicked a flower pot all across the yard."

"He ate four cream puffs all by himself."

"He says he's our boss and we are his servants."

"How long will he be here, Mama?"

Julia drew her two daughters close. "I didn't know that it would be this hard," she admitted. "But we must do it. We must help Papa. Do you understand? It won't be long. In fact, they are so unhappy with our accommodations that they might not even stay." Seeing hope in the girls' eyes, Julia hurried on. "But we must try to keep them. Everyone is counting on us. We must do the best we can—the very best—to endure." [76–77]

We can only do our best, and only God can do the rest.

And labour, working with our own hands: being reviled, we
bless; being persecuted, we suffer it.

1 CORINTHIANS 4:12

A GREATER LOSS

After they had gone to bed, Julia told John the news about the church. "John, we can't let the church go. We just can't. We need it. Our children need it. The whole town needs it."

John nodded in agreement. "So how can we save it?"

"We have to increase the attendance."

"Jule, folks have moved, and there is nothing to bring them back."

"I'm talking about the ones who are still here," said Julia. "There must be thirty or so still in town. That would be enough to keep a church open, don't you think?"

"It would if they all went to church, but they don't. They only go on special occasions. How can we change that?"

"They need the church," Julia insisted. "More than ever, they need the church. I don't know how they manage to get along without it—without God. Especially now that things are so hard. How do they get by without prayer, John? What do they do when they need answers? I haven't been doing my job," said Julia softly. "Here I am, trying to save their homes, their possessions, their— their way of life—and I haven't even been thinking about saving their souls." [109]

God is more concerned about saving our lives
than about saving our lifestyles.

For what shall it profit a man, if he shall gain the whole world, and lose his own soul?

MARK 8:36

81

FINDING GOD

There was silence again as John thought about Julia's words.

"I don't know why I didn't realize it earlier," she continued. "For—for some reason I—I guess I thought that believing—going to church—trying to live right—was enough. It's not, John. Not when your neighbors don't know—don't understand about God."

John drew her close. "We'll pray, Jule," he said softly, "for the people who are left. Maybe there is still something we can do for them. We might not be able to help them find work, but maybe we can help them find God."

[109–110]

Finding a job without finding God
may lead to a false sense of security.

Seek ye first the kingdom of God, and his righteousness; and all these things shall be added unto you.

MATTHEW 6:33

SPIRITUAL HUNGER

How to save the church topped Julia's list of concerns. *We need the church so people will have a chance to hear the Gospel,* she kept telling herself. She organized a meeting and sent out personal invitations for Sunday services. Then she arranged special events for the children during Sunday school.

The response was not good. Few people seemed to notice. They seemed no more interested in the church than they had in the past.

"I don't know what else to do," Julia confided to John.

"I'll talk to the pastor," John promised. "Perhaps he has some ideas."

But Pastor Wright had no ideas either. "We have tried and tried to get the people interested," he sighed. "There just doesn't seem to be any concern for spiritual things."

John talked to some of the men, trying to convince them that letting the church close was as bad as having the mill shut down. But the blank stares he got in response told him the men had no idea what he was talking about. They did not understand why anyone would worry about religion when just getting food on the table consumed all their energies. They did not consider spiritual needs as important as physical needs. [114–115]

> *An empty stomach makes life on earth unpleasant,*
> *but an empty heart makes life in heaven impossible.*

Whosoever drinketh of the water that I shall give him shall never thirst. JOHN 4:14

SPREADING THE WORD

Julia felt heavy with sorrow as she watched the Wrights depart. The townspeople needed the Gospel. How would they hear it now that their church had been taken from them?

Julia and John felt the urgency to do something. They needed spiritual nurturing. Their children needed biblical training. Their neighbors all needed it too, though none seemed to realize it.

"We'll just have to start our own Bible study," John decided. "We'll gather those who are interested and have our own service."

"Where?" asked Julia, eager to get started.

John thought for a few minutes. "Not in the church. People have shied away from church in the past. Perhaps—perhaps if we have it here, like you do the committee meetings, folks might get the notion to come."

Julia nodded, her eyes beginning to shine. "Do you really think it might work?"

"Might. We'll never know 'til we try." [117–119]

The spread of the Gospel does not depend on a building with open doors so that unbelievers can come in but on believers with open hearts who are willing to go out.

Go ye therefore, and teach all nations, baptizing them in the name of the Father, and of the Son, and of the Holy Ghost: Teaching them to observe all things whatsoever I have commanded you: and, lo, I am with you alway, *even* unto the end of the world. MATTHEW 28:19–20

FREE TO SERVE

After breakfast, Julia set to work writing invitations to a Bible study and sent Jennifer and Felicity to deliver them.

Only the Adams family and Hettie and Tom came to the first meeting. John read the Scriptures and discussed the lesson. Those who wished to pray did so, and the meeting ended.

Julia kept her initial disappointment to herself, but she didn't remain disappointed for long. As the winter weeks passed, a few others joined them for worship. Mrs. Greenwald came first. Julia wondered if she came out of boredom or curiosity. Then Mrs. Shannon came, and soon she was bringing her children. Julia decided they needed a lesson for the children, so she started a children's class. Soon the news got around and other children began coaxing their parents to allow them to attend. The class grew, and Julia assigned the younger ones to Jennifer and Felicity. Excited about being involved, the girls prepared lessons with great care.

The group grew and interest deepened. There was actually participation—excitement. Julia and John began to pray more sincerely. Perhaps this was why God had kept them in town—to win their neighbors. [119]

Those who choose to be servants
know the most about being free.

For though I be free from all *men*, yet have I made myself servant unto all, that I might gain the more.

1 CORINTHIANS 9:19

Anna raised her head and looked into Julia's eyes. "You know, don't you? That something is—is wrong between—"

"I guessed," said Julia softly. "Would you like to talk about it?"

"It's just—just—well, it isn't what I expected it to be."

"It never is," responded Julia. "We expect romance, flowers, love songs," said Julia. "Instead, we get dirty dishes, laundry, and silence."

"But I thought—"

"And he thought," said Julia. "I suppose he expected things like welcome-home kisses, his favorite pie, and slippers. Instead, he got broken plumbing, mounting bills, and complaints. If only there were some way to prepare for reality rather than romance," Julia went on, "marriage would have a much better chance."

"Are you saying there is no romance?"

"Oh, my, no! There is romance. Our problem is that we want it all to be romance. In reality we must first know each other, learn from each other, protect and support each other. We must build together. Work together. And then we experience the real romance—the excitement of fulfillment and shared love. More exciting than we ever dreamed." [126–127]

> *When we work together to clear the brambles we'll*
> *eventually uncover the fragrant roses.*

According to the effectual working in the measure of every part, maketh increase of the body unto the edifying of itself in love.   EPHESIANS 4:16

NURTURING LOVE

Julia leaned from the swing and plucked a flower from the nearby bush. "See this rosebud?" She held it out to Anna. "It's perfect. So new, so full of promise and color. Someday it will be a full flower. Beautiful, fragrant. But just suppose I want it that way now. So I take the petals and force them to open up, to be mature—now. What will happen?"

Anna waited.

"I'd spoil it," Julia said. "I would crush and bruise it, and it would just wilt and die. It takes time to reach full-flower," Julia continued. "We must nurture love, not rush it. If we are patient, it will bloom."

[127–128]

Love can't grow to its full potential
if it's planted in barren hearts.

Love covereth all sins.

PROVERBS 10:12

WAITING ON GOD

John was not sleeping well. In spite of his faith, his mind was troubled. Things were not going as planned. They'd had only one paying customer so far this season. All of the reserve money was gone.

The garden had been good again. John breathed a prayer of thanks for that. But even so, they needed many items the garden could not produce.

There was also the matter of the girls' education. Another school year was drawing near. The girls needed more than Jule could teach them at home. They were quickly becoming young women, and John and Julia wanted them to have a proper education—perhaps college if they were interested.

John shifted under the blankets, unable to find a comfortable position. Beside him, Julia breathed evenly.

Oh, God, he prayed silently as he had many times before, *please show me what to do. It would break Jule's heart to leave here—this house. I could never offer her a house like this again. But we can't go on living like this—no income to speak of—nor much hope of any—and so many needs for the family. Help me too, when I talk to Jule about our future. Give me the right words. Oh, God! I need you so much!* [129–130]

> When we have the right motives
> we will eventually do the right thing.

Lead me in thy truth, and teach me: for thou *art* the God of my salvation; on thee do I wait all the day.

PSALM 25:5

Good news," called Julia. "We are having more guests."

John decided to say nothing to dampen her spirit even though he knew it would take many more guests to meet the family's growing needs. He forced a smile. "When?" he asked.

"Monday!" exclaimed Julia. "Next Monday. A couple—and two girls—grown girls. They plan on a couple of weeks but may stay longer if they like it. They'll like it. It's so—so beautiful here." Julia gazed at the sweeping valley with the silver curve of the river, the shimmer of the distant lake, the slopes of nearby mountains rising up to join rugged crags and rocky peaks still covered by glacial ice.

"That's great!" John responded, trying to make his emotions match his words.

"Isn't it? I've been praying and praying—and here is our answer. Oh, John, this venture has been so difficult at times—but it has been a time of growing too. I have been shown over and over how God answers prayer. He never lets us down, John. Just when I think we can't make it any more, He answers my prayer again. And—He's never late. Though at times I think He's going to be."

John turned away to gaze at the distant peaks. *Oh, God,* he prayed silently, *I wish I had Jule's faith.* [134–135]

Even though we can't know God's timetable,
we can trust His timing.

And let us not be weary in well doing: for in due season we shall reap, if we faint not.

GALATIANS 6:9

HELD BY GOD

What do you think Jesus meant by these words?" John asked the group.

"I've been sittin' here, puzzling over them," admitted Mrs. Adams. "Perhaps He means, what we try to keep—try to hang on to—can still slip from us. What we honestly, openly, give to Him, He somehow keeps for us—and might even one day allow us to have back."

"Isn't He talking about our lives too?" added Mr. Adams. "If we refuse to give our life to Him, try to hang on to it for our own pleasures and self-seeking, we will eventually lose it. We will have no future with Him in heaven."

"I think you are both right," said Mrs. Shannon. "He's talking about our lives—but the same principle applies to other things too. We can never hold tight to anything. We haven't the strength—nor the power to keep it. Nothing—nothing in this life is safe from destruction and decay. Take our town here—our jobs. Even our lives. We can't save anything by our determination—no matter how we try." [138]

What God gives to us no one can take away;
what we withhold from God none of us can keep.

Whosoever shall seek to save his life shall lose it; and whosoever shall lose his life shall preserve it.

LUKE 17:33

FOLLOWING GOD

M r. and Mrs. Adams have been church people for years," Mrs. Greenwald reminded the group. "They know when God speaks. But what about the rest of us? Like me and—well, I won't mention any other names, but how do we know when God speaks, when we have never asked for, never looked for, His leading?"

The stillness hung heavy in the room. "I wouldn't have known—a few years ago," said Victor Adams. "A person needs to walk with God, to pray and read the Word, before he can know when God speaks and where He is leading. You might need to take that important first step toward God—accept Him as Savior—before you can hear Him speak to you, Mrs. Greenwald."

John was quick to seize the opportunity. "Would you like to come into the east parlor?" he asked. "We'll show you how you can take that first step—to become a child of God."

She nodded.

[140]

The first thing God says to every person is "Follow me."

For God so loved the world, that he gave his only begotten Son, that whosoever believeth in him should not perish, but have everlasting life.   JOHN 3:16

SPIRITUAL TRADE-INS

I've wanted to become God's child for a long time," said Mrs. Greenwald, "but I didn't know how to go about it. And I was scared to death to go to the parson. I was afraid he would want an account of every sin I ever committed and there are—were—so many of them."

Julia knew that their former pastor would have demanded no such thing, but folks often had funny ideas about preachers.

"I had no idea that I could go directly to God—in Jesus' name—and ask forgiveness," the woman went on.

"That's how we each must do it," said Julia, giving her a warm embrace.

"Well, it's a big relief, I'll tell you that."

They rejoined the group in the main parlor. Julia noticed people watching Mrs. Greenwald. They were curious as to what had happened and if it had really "worked." If Mrs. Greenwald was conscious of the attention, she did not let on. She hugged each of her children, then turned to greet her neighbors with a shining face. "I don't know why I didn't do this years ago," she told them.   [141]

> Satan would have us believe that God takes things away
> when we give ourselves to Him. The truth is that God
> gives so many good, new gifts that we willingly
> abandon our old rusty possessions.

Therefore if any man *be* in Christ, *he is* a new creature: old things are passed away; behold, all things are become new.

2 CORINTHIANS 5:17

REPENTANCE

W hat a wonderful day," Julia said to the family at dinner. "Imagine! Mrs. Greenwald is the first convert of our worship services. I don't think she ever would have gone to church. Here I was praying to keep the church open, and there she was with a hungry heart but too stubborn—or afraid—to go to the services. God knew what He was doing all the time in closing the doors of the church."

"But, Mama," spoke Felicity, "what if there are others who would go to church, but won't come here?"

"I—really don't know," Julia admitted. "Maybe I said it all wrong. Maybe God didn't speak to Mrs. Greenwald because the church closed its doors. Maybe He had to use our group because the church had closed. Maybe that was the only way He could get our—my—attention. Suddenly I realized that I had an obligation. Before, I had left it all to the church. To the minister. I shouldn't have. If I had been as concerned when the church was still here as I am now—well, the church might still be open."

It was a sobering thought for Julia. She knew she had failed in her Christian commitment. She had waited too long to express concern for her neighbors.

[141–142]

God doesn't expect perfection,
but He does expect repentance.

For godly sorrow worketh repentance to salvation.

2 CORINTHIANS 7:10

JUDGING OTHERS

Miss Constance, one of the new guests, rapped on the kitchen door to say that Miss Priscilla was ready for tea.

"I'll send it right up," Julia promised.

"No need for you to run up with it. I'll take it."

Looking up in surprise, Julia saw eyes full of deep sorrow. She wanted to pull the young woman into her arms, but instead she turned her attention to the task at hand.

"My," remarked Julia, when the door had closed, "have you ever seen a sadder looking face?"

"She's awfully quiet," said Felicity.

"She was quiet in the parlor too," Jennifer added. "I never heard her say one thing over tea. Did you, Mama?"

"No, I guess I didn't," admitted Julia.

"The mother—now she prattled the whole time," Jennifer explained to Felicity. "I don't know who she was talking to. No one was listening. But she talked without stopping."

"Don't judge too soon," cautioned Julia, "or too harshly. We really don't know anything about them yet." [151–152]

If we are honest about what is in our own hearts
we won't have the audacity to judge others
for what we think is in theirs.

Judge not, and ye shall not be judged: condemn not, and ye
shall not be condemned: forgive, and ye shall be forgiven.

LUKE 6:37

PEACE WITH GOD

Julia wired her father, and his return message revealed that his excitement at having his granddaughters visit more than matched that of the girls.

As Julia worked anxiously to prepare her daughters for a time with their grandfather, her tears often fell on the fabric. She hoped with all her heart that the three would fall in love. She hoped her father understood her great love for him as she sent to him her most precious possessions. She hoped too that her girls would see in him all of the goodness, kindness, and wisdom she had always found. Julia prayed and prayed as she stitched. Her papa, whom she loved dearly, had not yet made his peace with God.

The time is getting short, Julia often reminded herself as she had reminded him in the past. But whenever she wrote to him of her concern, his return letters responded to every part of her letter except the paragraphs about his spiritual condition.

Perhaps Jennifer . . . Julia thought. *She shared her faith with Millicent. Perhaps she will be able to explain her faith to her grandfather—in her own simple way.* The thought made Julia pray even more diligently.

[171]

We may have to give a piece of ourselves
so that others can find peace with God.

The Lord is . . . not willing that any should perish, but that all should come to repentance.

2 PETER 3:9

95

THE RIGHT THING

And then in a flurry the girls were gone. It happened all too quickly for Julia. One minute she was holding her two daughters; the next minute the train was chugging away, leaving her empty and alone. She watched the white handkerchiefs waving from the windows until they were out of sight.

Then she turned to John and let the tears flow freely. He held her tightly, wishing with all his heart that he didn't have to leave the next day.

Julia soon straightened and looked into his eyes.

"We have done the right thing?" She worded it as statement but pronounced it as a question.

John patted her shoulder. "We have done the right thing," he declared, and Julia found comfort in his reply.   [172]

Doing the right thing
is seldom an easy thing to do.

For as the sufferings of Christ abound in us, so our consolation also aboundeth by Christ.

2 CORINTHIANS 1:5

BEING USED

Julia burst into the kitchen, her eyes snapping. Then she lowered herself into a chair as if her legs would not hold her a moment longer. "Miss Priscilla!" exclaimed Julia, "she's—she's with child!"

"I suspected," said Hettie as she continued to peel potatoes.

"Well, I never! Who would have thought of such—The very idea—using my house—my Christian home—as a—a hideaway. Well, I won't have it! Not in my house. I will not hide a woman who—who lived immorally and went sneaking off to hide her sin. Why did she pick us? Why did she come here? There must be other places, but no. She had to choose us."

"Maybe she didn't choose us," Hettie responded.

"What are you trying to say, Hettie?" Julia asked.

"The woman is a sinner—just like you said," Hettie answered softly. "How did our Lord feel about sinners?"

Julia's eyes grew big. Her head dropped. "Oh, Hettie," she repented, "I just never thought—" There was silence again while Julia did some soul searching. At last she lifted her head. "Do you think God sent her here for us to—to help—to love?" [176–177]

When we feel as if we're being used by other people,
it may be an opportunity to be used by God.

But I say unto you which hear, Love your enemies, do good
to them which hate you, Bless them that curse you, and pray
for them which despitefully use you.

LUKE 6:27–28

SURVIVAL

John strolled the short distance from the eating area to the shack. He wanted time to think—to pray. It was nearly impossible to pray with the raucous laughter, coarse jokes, and smoke-filled air pressing in on him. He stepped off the beaten path and lowered himself onto a fallen log. The night sky was clear, and stars were beginning to appear. John was weary. It had been a long, hard day of heavy work in the woods. At least the physical exhaustion kept him from thinking too many painful thoughts and made it easy for him to sleep at night despite his many concerns. And of course he was glad to have a paycheck coming regularly. John turned his face toward heaven as his chest tightened with loneliness. Jule. The girls. Even the familiarity of his small town. He missed it all very much.

"God," he whispered into the night, "I'm glad I didn't need to leave you behind too." He sat silently, unable to go on. He watched the moon rise over the nearby pines. In the forest a wolf howled and another responded. They were on the hunt. They needed to survive. John felt a kinship with the wolves. He too was fighting for survival. For himself—but mostly for Jule. For the girls. He had to survive—for them.   [181–182]

> *Struggling so that others can survive*
> *gives us the strength and will to survive ourselves.*

I have shewed you all things, how that so labouring ye ought
to support the weak, and to remember the words of the Lord
Jesus, how he said, It is more blessed to give than to receive.

ACTS 20:35

THE FATHERLESS

Baby boy Blakeney was eventually dressed in a white gown with pink ribbons, bundled in used pink blankets, and laid in an emptied, towel-padded dresser drawer. Julia could have wept as she looked down on him.

"You poor little soul," she whispered. "You didn't ask to come into the world. And you certainly didn't get much of a welcome. What will happen to you? If only I could have had you to love—" Julia brushed away tears and went back to the kitchen to prepare hot tea for Miss Priscilla.

They had nothing for the new baby. Tom fashioned a nipple of sorts from the finger of a new glove. It was all Mr. Perry had in his store that would make any kind of feeding arrangement. Julia fixed a bottle of milk and fed the hungry baby.

Constance took over the care of the infant as Julia instructed her. There were no diapers, so Julia had Hettie tear up an old flannel sheet. There wasn't even time to put in a proper hem.

Julia had never before felt so disturbed over the birth of a baby. Her heart cried, *It's not right, It's not fair. He wasn't at fault.* It seemed so totally wrong that a child should be born unwanted— unwelcomed—unloved. [189]

No child is born unwanted, but sometimes the people who
want them aren't the ones who give them birth.

Thou art the helper of the fatherless.

PSALM 10:14

WILLING TO BE FOOLISH

Three heads lifted and three pairs of eyes studied the man's face.

"What do you mean?" asked Constance.

"I need clothes and food for the infant," the doctor repeated. "Enough for a twelve-hour trip. Why is that confusing?"

"But you can't take the baby."

"I must take the baby—I have a contract," the man declared.

"Oh, Constance. For goodness' sake don't fuss," broke in Priscilla, tossing her napkin on the table and standing up. "You know the plan—the arrangement. Mother has it all cared for."

"But I love him!" Constance shouted at her sister. "I love him."

Priscilla looked at Constance. Surprise and anger flashed across her face. Then she began to cry. "You will not bring that—that baby home. Do you hear? You will not!"

Julia trembled. She had never witnessed such a quarrel. She wanted to cover her ears and flee, but she was rooted to the spot.

"Of course I won't take him home!" Constance shouted back at her sister. "I wouldn't dream of taking him to—to that place."

"You're a fool!" yelled Priscilla. "You're a—a pigheaded, selfish fool." [191–192]

*We may be considered foolish for loving an unwanted child,
but we'll never be wrong.*

Defend the poor and fatherless: do justice to the afflicted and needy.   PSALM 82:3

Constance turned her face away as Julia spoke.

"Just think of it, Constance. Somewhere—right now—there is a very excited woman—and man—waiting for that little one. Can you imagine how they feel?"

Constance made no effort to respond. Julia stepped closer and placed her hand on the trembling shoulder.

"Constance, I am not trying to make it harder for you. I just want you to think about the other couple. How they might have prayed—longed for a baby. Little Peter could—will—make them very happy. He is such a sweet little thing. He will be loved. We'll pray for that. We'll pray that he has wise and kind and loving parents."

Constance whispered, "You are right. He is better off with—with both a mother and father. I loved him—will always love him—but I couldn't have given him the home he deserved. Oh, Julia, I need to learn how to pray so that I might pray for him. I know you know how. I have watched you—with me—with Priscilla. No one could have been as kind or as patient without—without a deep faith in God. Please—please tell me what I must do to find God in that way."   [194]

Anger draws people's attention to us;
gentleness draws people's attention to God.

The discretion of a man deferreth his anger; and *it is* his glory
to pass over a transgression.

PROVERBS 19:11

101

OVERCOMING EVIL

Priscilla and Constance left the next day. "I will write," Constance promised Julia. "Thank you. Thank you so much—for sharing your faith—for understanding—for your love."

Julia hugged her and blinked back tears. She turned from Constance to Priscilla. The train was coming toward them, chugging heavily as it pulled up the incline toward the station.

"Priscilla," said Julia. "I—I'll continue to pray for you." Julia tried to give the girl a parting embrace, but Priscilla accepted only a token hug and then stepped back quickly.

"Constance, grab that big bag," she ordered, "it's much too heavy for me."

Julia turned back to Constance who welcomed the warmth of her farewell embrace.

"Don't let her upset you," whispered Constance. "She was affected by your love much more than she lets on. She said as much to me. And now that I know God—I will be able to help her. I will keep working and praying and—who knows?" [195]

The harvest of love and kindness sown on earth
won't be weighed until heaven.

Therefore if thine enemy hunger, feed him; if he thirst, give him drink: for in so doing thou shalt heap coals of fire on his head. Be not overcome of evil, but overcome evil with good.

ROMANS 12:20–21

GIVING UP

John led Julia to the porch swing and motioned for her to be seated. He eased himself down beside her. "Jule," he began slowly, "I've been doing a lot of thinking." He paused to choose his words carefully. He did not want to hurt the woman he loved so dearly. "I'm afraid we are going to have to give up, Jule. To let the house go." John waited, holding his breath. He expected a cry of protest, but Julia remained silent. "We can't go on like this. I can't stand being without you—without the girls. We need to be together. To be a family again. I know it will hurt you to lose the house, but—"

"The house?" gasped Julia. "You think I can't give up the house? John, I don't care about the house. Without my family the big, beautiful house has become a mammoth tomb. Empty and lonely. It isn't my love for the house that has kept me here, John. It's my love for you. I thought you couldn't bear to give up the house."

"You mean—?"

Julia nodded vigorously. "You worked so hard to give me everything—to have things perfect for me. I thought it would crush you to give it all up. I tried to hold it for you," sobbed Julia, burying her face against her husband's shoulder.

"Oh, Jule, Jule," John soothed. "I just want you. I want us to be together." [202–203]

> *Only when we are willing to give up what we have gained*
> *can we gain what we love.*

I seek not yours, but you. . . . And I will very gladly spend and be spent for you. 2 CORINTHIANS 12:14–15

John kissed Julia, his face sobering. "I was so afraid you might not want to go off to another lumber town. That you wouldn't be able to leave—this." He nodded toward the large white house.

Julia shook her head with confidence. She was surprised that her troubled mind felt peace at last.

"It's time," she whispered. "I feel—feel free to go now. I didn't feel this way before. Why?"

"Perhaps because you were still needed here," John answered.

Julia thought of Constance. "Yes, perhaps that is the reason," she said. "Maybe I was still needed here."

"And now?" asked John.

Julia placed her arms around his neck, her face aglow. "Now," she said, "now God is giving us new challenges. New adventures. Oh, John! I'm so thankful we can face them together." [204]

We can face the future with confidence
when we've been obedient in the past.

Trust in the Lord with all thine heart; and lean not unto thine own understanding. In all thy ways acknowledge him, and he shall direct thy paths.

PROVERBS 3:5–6

Roses for Mama

JOY IN LABOR

Angela Peterson wiped her hands on her dark blue apron, then reached up and tucked a wisp of blond hair into a side comb. It was a warm day, and the tub of hot water over which she had been leaning did not make it any cooler. She stretched to take some of the kink from her back and lifted her eyes to the back field where Thomas's breaking plow stitched a furrowed pattern. He would soon be in for his dinner.

Angela bent over the tub again and scrubbed the soiled socks with renewed vigor. She wanted to finish before stopping to put dinner on the table, and this was her last load.

"I hate washing socks," she fretted, then quickly bit her tongue as she recalled a soft voice: "Remember, never despise a task—any task. In doing any job, you are either creating something or bettering something." [11]

If we learn to find joy in doing a job well,
we can have joy in any job we do.

A man hath no better thing under the sun, than to eat, and to drink, and to be merry: for that shall abide with him of his labour the days of his life, which God giveth him under the sun.　　ECCLESIASTES 8:15

Is it warm enough to plant the garden yet?" asked Angela.

"I'll get it ready for you—but I'd give it a few more days," said Thomas. "I don't like the feel of the wind today. It could blow in another storm."

Angela could smell the stew and quickly rose to check. A look into the pot showed her that it was bubbling. She stirred it again on the way to the serving bowl she had placed on the table. She could hear the coffee boiling too, but it was Thomas who moved to lift the pot from the hot stove. Without comment he filled their cups and returned the pot to the back of the stove.

"Mrs. Owens was planting her garden yesterday when I went in to town," Angela commented as she placed the empty stew pot on the cupboard and took her chair at the table.

"Mrs. Owens plants a couple times each spring," replied Thomas, lowering himself to his chair. "She always gets caught by frost. 'No patience,' Papa used to say."

[14]

If we disregard God's laws of nature, we'll never harvest any fruit. If we disregard God's laws of human nature, we'll never harvest any goodness.

To every *thing there is* a season, and a time to every purpose under the heaven: A time to be born, and a time to die; a time to plant, and a time to pluck up *that which is* planted.

ECCLESIASTES 3:1–2

RESPONSE TO OTHERS

Derek said nothing, but a red tinge began to flush his cheeks.

"Louise," reprimanded Angela gently, "don't tease your brother."

"Well, it's true. Marigold tried to sit beside him and everything."

Poor Derek, thought Angela. *So shy—and now this.* "Lots of girls like Thomas too," she countered. "I've watched them at church and at picnics. They try to get his attention in all sorts of ways. There's nothing wrong with having friends."

"But," argued Louise, trying to keep her announcement controversial, "Thomas is growed up."

"Grown up," corrected Angela. "Grown up."

"Derek is still just a kid."

"Kids need friends too," said Angela in Derek's defense.

"Well—not that kind. Not the kind Marigold wants to be. She smiles silly smiles and rolls her eyes and says, 'Oh-h-h,' like that, and all sorts of silly things."

"Derek is not responsible for the way Marigold acts," Angela said firmly. "He is only responsible for himself. Mama always said that true breeding is shown in how we respond to the foolishness of others," she finished, her voice softer. [17–18]

The way we respond to others
is evidence of how we respond to God.

It is an honour for a man to cease from strife.

PROVERBS 20:3

AUTHORITY

Why do you always say 'Change your school clothes and care for your chores'?" asked Louise, mimicking Angela.

"Because it always needs to be done," Angela responded simply.

"Don't you think we know that? We've been doing it ever since we started off to school—and I'm in fifth grade now."

Louise had never openly challenged Angela before, and she wasn't sure how to handle it. Nor was she sure how Mama would have handled it. She could not remember ever having challenged Mama, and none of the others were old enough to defy Mama before—

"That's naughty," Sara was saying to Louise. "We're s'pose to 'bey Angela."

"She's not our mama," Louise said in a defiant whisper.

"Well—she has to take care of us," Derek managed in a weak voice. "And you know what Thomas would say if he heard you talking sass."

Louise flipped her braids. "And Thomas is not our papa," she responded, repeating the challenge.

"We don't got a mama and papa anymore," cut in Sara insistently. "Angela and Thomas are all we got." [18–19]

God expects more from the one in authority
than the one under authority.

Obey them that have the rule over you, and submit yourselves: for they watch for your souls, as they that must give account.   HEBREWS 13:17

FAMILY TIES

Angela tried to calm her trembling soul as she poured the milk. She had an ordeal ahead of her and she wasn't sure how to handle it. None of the children had ever challenged her authority before. What was she to do—and how often in the future might she need to face the same crisis?

Oh, God, she prayed silently. *Help me with this. What should I do? I've noticed little hints of tension—but this—this open defiance—I have no idea—* Her voice trembled as she spoke to Derek. "Thomas would like you to check the south fence. He doesn't want the cows getting out. I'll have Louise and Sara help with some of your other chores so you won't be working after dark."

"What do I have to do?" asked Sara.

"Well, you can feed the hens and gather the eggs as usual; then you can help Louise fill the wood box."

"What if Louise doesn't want to?" questioned Sara as she dipped her cookie into her milk.

Angela hesitated. "Louise is a part of this family," she finally said. "We all must share in the work. I'm afraid she will have to do her share of chores—whether she wants to or not." [19–20]

> *If children give nothing to the family when they're young they'll have no ties to it when they're older.*

From whom the whole body fitly joined together . . . according to the effectual working in the measure of every part, maketh increase of the body unto the edifying of itself in love.   EPHESIANS 4:16

RESISTING AUTHORITY

Angela delayed her talk with Louise as long as she could and then went slowly toward the closed door, praying silently with every step. She found Louise seated calmly on the chair by the bed reading from her favorite book. She had changed into her chore clothes and had neatly hung her school garments.

"Louise," spoke Angela, "I think we need to talk a bit. Perhaps I do tell you over and over again what I expect you to do. I still need to tell Sara. She hasn't heard it as often as you—and, well, when I am telling one it is just easier to include all of you."

Louise nodded, no defiance in her eyes now.

"I'm sorry," Angela said softly. "I'll try to remember that you are responsible enough to know to look after your usual duties." She sat down on the bed near her younger sister and took her hand.

"Louise," she said gently, "you know that before Mama died she asked me to care for all of you. I told her I would. Mama felt strongly that caring was more than putting food on the table and seeing that clothes were washed and mended. Mama wants each of us to grow to be strong, good, dependable. Part of that comes by sharing chores—and learning obedience. It won't always be easy to have an older sister be your authority—but that's the way it is. Not by our choosing, but that's the way it is." [20–21]

To resist God's choice of authority over us
is to put more faith in ourselves than in God.

Whosoever therefore resisteth the power, resisteth the ordinance of God.   ROMANS 13:2

DISCIPLINE & LOVE

I always thought raising the children would get easier with the passing of time," Angela said to Thomas. "But it hasn't. When they were little it was just a case of feeding them and looking after their clothes and loving them a lot. But now all the years without Mama to guide them—to teach them how to treat others, how to show respect and obedience—that's what they've missed, Thomas."

"You've been giving them that," Thomas assured Angela. "At the last church picnic I heard some of the ladies talking about what fine kids they are and what good manners they have and—"

Angela was pleased to hear the comment, but she knew that much more than "please" and "thank you" was involved in properly raising children.

"They have proper conduct on the outside," Angela agreed. "But on the inside? All the things Mama taught—about thinking of others—about not letting little hurts make one into a complainer—about seeing beauty in simple things—about so many things. I'm afraid I haven't been getting some of those lessons across. I'm not even sure how Mama did it. I just know that those thoughts—those feelings are deep inside of me—and they came from Mama." [24–25]

Discipline will change children's behavior;
but only love can change their attitudes and motives.

Even a child is known by his doings, whether his work *be* pure, and whether *it be* right.

PROVERBS 20:11

THE BEST TIME

ngela realized Thomas was right about Derek. "What can we do?" she wondered out loud.

"I've been thinking. Maybe I should take Derek fishing—or something."

Angela unfolded her tense hands and reached out to touch Thomas's sleeve. "That's a wonderful idea!" she exclaimed. "When?"

"Well, I don't know—exactly. I've got to get the crop in and then—"

"Thomas, I don't think you should wait. Not until you have everything done. You know how it is. On a farm there is always something that needs doing. You'll never find the time if you wait for it all to be done."

"Well, I can't just up and leave the work while I run off to—"

"Why not? The kids are more important than anything else. I know that's what Mama would say. She would want you to go. At least for a couple of days—even an afternoon if that's all you can manage. We need to be—to be putting first things first. I mean— what good is the farm if—?"   [28–29]

When we know the right thing to do,
to delay doing it is wrong.

When thou vowest a vow unto God, defer not to pay it.

ECCLESIASTES 5:4

LOVING GOD

Nothing much had changed, but Angela's load had lifted by the time she returned to the kitchen. She still had to raise her brother and two sisters, but she had Thomas to help her, to share the responsibilities. At least they were planning now—trying to do more than just feed and clothe their siblings.

"I must take more time to do things with the girls," she said, more to herself than to Thomas. "All I have been doing is handing out orders. 'Do this. Don't do that.' They need time to be children. I need to find ways to teach them. Encourage them. Just like Mama did with me."

Thomas placed a hand on her shoulder. "Don't be too hard on yourself, Angie," he cautioned. "Don't set the standards impossibly high. You're human too, you know."

Thomas turned to bolt the door behind them. In the semidarkness he looked like Pa. She had never noticed the likeness before. Her pa would be so proud of his son. Thomas had been almost raised before they had lost their parents. If only—if only she could bring the others up to deserve family pride too. If only they would grow up to be responsible members of society. If only they would grow up to love God.

[29–30]

*If we teach children to be good citizens they won't
necessarily love God, but if we teach them to
love God they will be good citizens.*

Come, ye children, hearken unto me: I will teach you the
fear of the Lord.   PSALM 34:11

LIVING OUR FAITH

The dearest and closest friends of the orphaned Peterson children were the Andrewses. Mr. Andrews operated the town mercantile, the store where Angela did the family shopping. He was a soft-spoken man, as good at living out his religion as declaring it. Few people could find anything disparaging to say about Mr. Andrews without embellishing it with untruths. He was not interfering, but each member of the Peterson family knew that if ever a need arose, Mr. Andrews was the man to whom they should go.

Mrs. Andrews was a motherly woman who had little to say but whose smile welcomed everyone. And her instincts seemed always to be right. She passed out cookies and hugs with abandon. Even Thomas, big and strapping as he was, accepted his share, and Angela felt that some of her days were made endurable because of the embrace of the kind woman. [34]

One good way to live our faith
is to freely give a warm embrace.

Put on therefore, as the elect of God, holy and beloved, bowels of mercies, kindness, humbleness of mind, meekness, longsuffering.

COLOSSIANS 3:12

BETRAYED

On the night of Trudie's party Angela noticed Thomas fussing over his shoes and hair. He spent more time before the kitchen basin slicking down his wayward cowlick than Angela spent pinning up her own tresses. Angela tried not to let him see that she was noticing, but she did wonder about it.

They walked together toward Trudie's and took a short-cut across the neighbors' field. Thomas had a hard time slowing his stride to accommodate Angela. She had never seen him so eager before. *Perhaps he has been missing fun,* she reasoned.

Trudie met them at the gate. She reached a hand to Angela, but it was Thomas who got her full attention.

"I'm so glad you could come," she said, her voice soft and warm, and Angela felt a funny little trickle of fear run down her spine.

Trudie out to win Thomas? Could it be? It was Thomas she wanted all along, Angela suddenly realized. *She didn't care about me at all. She just wanted me to get Thomas here.*

Angela felt betrayed. Rejected. And terribly annoyed with Trudie—even with Thomas. Thomas was smiling back at Trudie. He even allowed her to take his arm and draw him toward the circle of friends. Angela seemed to have been forgotten. [40–41]

It is inevitable that others will turn away from us,
but it is certain that God will not.

Blessed *be* God, which hath not turned away my prayer, nor
his mercy from me. PSALM 66:20

FEAR OF LOSS

Angela felt someone take hold of her arm. She was hardly in the mood to be civil, much less friendly.

"Glad you could come," said Thane's familiar voice.

Angela was relieved. If Thomas wasn't planning to be with her it would be a comfort to have Thane nearby. But her eyes still followed Trudie and Thomas. Trudie hung on to Thomas's arm as though her life depended on it, and Thomas did not seem to object. What if Trudie was successful in wooing Thomas? Who would run the farm? Help raise the children? Surely Thomas would see through her ploy and let Trudie know in no uncertain terms that he was not interested. But Thomas was still smiling at Trudie and responding to her playful glances with animated conversation.

Thane guided Angela toward a small group of young people, and soon she was included in the circle and made to feel welcome. Now and then throughout the evening she glanced at Thomas. Trudie was never far from his side. Angela tried to push aside the nagging fear. Thomas belonged to the family. He was hers—had always been hers. They had been together ever since their pa and ma had left them. They bolstered each other, encouraged each other, cheered each other. If she should lose Thomas, she wasn't sure she would be able to carry on. [41–42]

What belongs to God we need not fear losing.

For I the Lord thy God will hold thy right hand, saying unto thee, Fear not; I will help thee.

ISAIAH 41:13

IN DUE SEASON

Thane knew Angela well. "You're angry about something," he stated. "Not just worried about the kids. What happened?"

Angela's chin quivered despite her attempts to still it. "Did you see Trudie? She was hanging on to Thomas like she owned him."

Thane chuckled. "Maybe she would like to."

"Well, she'd better back off."

"Why?" Thane asked. "I didn't see Tom objecting."

"Well, he should have. We need him here—with us. He isn't—"

"Wait a minute," said Thane, taking Angela by the shoulders. "Are you saying that you expect ol' Tom to just lay life aside and give all of his years to you?"

"Not me," choked Angela. "Not me. The kids need—"

"Angela," Thane broke in, "there might come a day when Tom will choose a life of his own. He has already postponed his own dreams. Is it right to expect him to forget all about them—forever?"

Angela wanted to lay her head against Thane's shoulder and let the tears fall, but she didn't. "I—I have to forget mine," she said, her voice trembling.

Thane answered slowly. "For now," he said. "For now. But may God grant that it might not always be so." [44]

If it hasn't happened, it isn't time.

And let us not be weary in well doing: for in due season we shall reap, if we faint not.

GALATIANS 6:9

119

WORRY

Angela returned from church having regained a measure of serenity. She still felt concern about rearing her siblings. She still felt a quiver of fear that Thomas might leave them for a life of his own, but she had balanced all of that with the fact that God did truly care about the Peterson family. Surely she didn't bear the burden of their welfare alone.

I must remember that, she chastised herself. If there ever was a lesson Mama emphasized it was that God loves them and would care for them. They only needed to trust Him.

The conversation around the dinner table that noon was of the usual sort. They spoke of the things they had heard that morning. They shared little stories about friends. Even Louise laughed at Thomas's silly jokes and joined in plans of "we should" or "could we?"

In fact, it seemed to Angela that things were back to normal again, and she began to wonder why she had allowed herself to get into such a stew. [50]

Worry is like fog: it has no power to hurt us, but if we move
too fast when we're in it we might hurt ourselves.

And which of you with taking thought can add to his stature one cubit? If ye then be not able to do that thing which is least, why take ye thought for the rest?

LUKE 12:25–26

120

CALLED TO BLESS

Mrs. Blackwell puffed her way up the veranda steps. "My, that sun is hot today" was the only greeting the woman offered. She whisked off her heavy black bonnet and wiped her perspiring face.

Angela stepped aside to let her enter the kitchen. She headed directly for a chair beside the table, her eyes surveying the room. "It's cool in here," she observed, "Guess you haven't been doin' any bakin' for a while."

"In hot weather I try to do enough in one day to last the week." Mrs. Blackwell wiped her face again and dropped heavily onto the chair. "How do you keep it fresh?" she probed.

"I wrap it and put it in the extra icebox in the shed out back."

The woman frowned. Angela knew Mrs. Blackwell had no spare icebox and was probably thinking it wasn't fair that someone so young should have things she didn't.

Angela turned to lift the teapot down from the shelf.

"You use that one for everyday? Looks to me like your mama would have kept thet for special occasions."

"Mama felt it a special occasion when a neighbor came to call," Angela answered sweetly, giving the woman a nice smile.   [66–67]

Gracious words show God's grace in us.

Not rendering evil for evil, or railing for railing: but contrariwise blessing; knowing that ye are thereunto called . . .   1 PETER 3:9

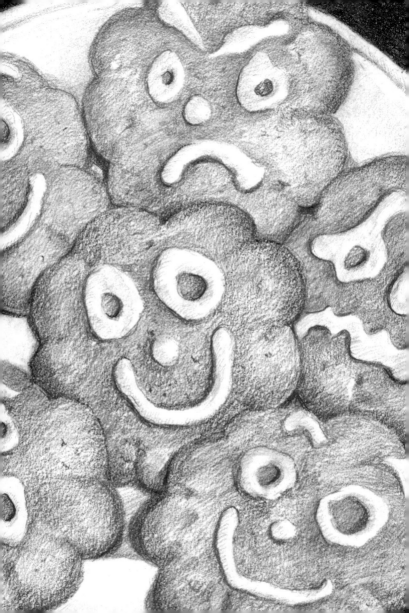

SIMPLE TRUTHS

The family's talk turned to childhood remembrances.

"Remember when Mama fixed us that little picnic and we ate it out in the yard under the bed sheets?" Angela asked.

"She pinned the sheets up to the clothesline," explained Thomas, "and then Pooch, that big oaf of a dog, came tearing around the corner of the house, afraid of the old sow or something, and ran smack into the side of it. It came down off the line and wrapped all around him and he ran off yapping like the world was coming to an end."

"And remember the time Mama made those cookies with the great big eyes and funny looks?" Thomas added. "Sad faces, happy faces, frowning faces, surprised faces. Then she put them on a plate and offered each of us one. We all picked a happy face. Remember? And then she said, 'Oh, look. You have all chosen a happy face. I guess everyone prefers a face that is happy. No one wants the sad or angry face. Let's change the rest.' And she did."

Angela nodded. Her mama had been so skillful at getting across simple lessons.

[50]

Simple truths, woven together,
strengthen the fabric of our character.

And these words, which I command thee this day, shall be in thine heart: And thou shalt teach them diligently unto thy children, and shalt talk of them when thou sittest in thine house, and when thou walkest by the way, and when thou liest down, and when thou risest up.

DEUTERONOMY 6:6–7

123

A MOTHER'S LESSONS

Tears came to Angela's eyes. She had worried that the younger children were forgetting their mother—had not had as many years to glean memories as she and Thomas had enjoyed. But she had not realized just how much they had been denied.

"You don't remember?" she asked.

Sara answered by shaking her head.

"You don't remember having Mama in the kitchen fixing after-school snacks? You don't remember the walks through her garden? You don't remember taking her hand to see the new calf?"

With each question Sara continued shaking her head.

"I remember a little bit," broke in Louise. "I remember the color of her hair. I even remember Papa calling it 'spun gold.' I remember her apron with the big pockets. And I remember one time when I scratched my knee and she fixed it—then she rocked me and sang me a song—about little birdies or something. I forget that part."

Angela was disturbed that her sisters had so few memories of their wonderful mother. No wonder it was so difficult for her to pass along to them all the lessons of proper conduct and correct attitudes.   [51]

A mother's lessons are a child's lifeline.

My son . . . forsake not the law of thy mother.
PROVERBS 1:8

124

MEMORIES

Do you remember Mama?" Angela asked, turning to look at Derek. The boy did not lift his eyes from his plate but nodded slightly. Angela saw him swallow. Her eyes misted as she wondered just what memories Derek had tucked away in his heart.

Angela responded quickly lest her emotions would overcome her, "Well, it is important for each of us to remember Mama and Papa. If you don't remember much about them, Thomas and I—and Derek—are going to have to share our memories. From now on we'll play a little game and the three of us will share memories about what they did—what they said—what they were like—so all of us will know them and have memories." [52]

Memories of the past help us keep
the proper perspective on the future.

The memory of the just *is* blessed.

PROVERBS 10:7

PREMATURE JUDGMENT

Angela was pleased to hear that Mr. Stratton's son had come to visit his ailing father. "I hope Mr. Stratton is well enough to enjoy the visit," she said.

"Gus didn't sound too excited about it," Thane continued. "I think he fears that the fellow is just interested in getting his hands on the Stratton money."

Angela was suddenly angry. Why couldn't it be concern—if not love—that was bringing the junior Stratton to his father's bedside?

"Well," she said defiantly, "perhaps Gus should wait and see before he brands the man. He could at least give him a chance. When is he to arrive?"

"Soon, I gather from what Gus said. He was spreading the word around town, though he was none too happy about the situation."

"That's awful," Angela said, still annoyed. "The poor man hasn't even done anything, and already folks are against him. Fine welcome for someone coming to see his sick pa."

Angela resolved that she would not be one to brand a man before she knew his intent. She promised herself she would take over some more baking the minute she learned of his arrival. [65–66]

When we form opinions based on speculation
we leave no room for truth.

Therefore judge nothing before the time, until the Lord come, who both will bring to light the hidden things of darkness, and will make manifest the counsels of the hearts.

1 CORINTHIANS 4:5

126

HURT

Derek's contributions to family memory time had become a bit more open, but Thomas and Angela knew he was still troubled.

"I remember—" began Derek, and then he swallowed hard, struggling to go on. "I remember—the day Mama died."

Angela caught her breath. Thomas reached out a hand to his young brother. "Yes?" he prompted.

"I brought her a bird shell—the baby had already hatched but I knew she would like to see it." He stopped and swallowed again. "I tiptoed into her bedroom. Then I touched her hand—it was cold. I—I whispered to her—but she didn't open her eyes. Then I—I shook her—just a little bit. Then I shook her harder—and she still didn't wake up. I got scared and started to cry. Then Mrs. Barrows opened the door and frowned at me. 'Your Mama is gone, boy,' she said. 'Mustn't cry, now. You're a big boy.' I ran past her and I ran and ran until I was out of breath and—"

Tears were falling freely down Derek's cheeks. Thomas held him closely. "That's right. Go ahead and cry it all out. I never heard Papa say that a man couldn't cry when he had good reason."

Oh, God, Angela prayed, *help poor little Derek. Wash his memory of this terrible hurt—and touch his soul with your healing. Might he be freed from the past now—and able to go on.*   [77–78]

Hurt concealed festers; hurt revealed heals.

I called upon the Lord in distress: the Lord answered me.

PSALM 118:5

GOD'S PLAN

Thane was quiet for a minute and then went on. "It doesn't seem too likely that I ever will farm, so I haven't said anything to anyone."

Angela nodded slowly and then reached out and took his arm. He gave her hand a slight squeeze in response.

"It's really strange, isn't it?" Angela said. "Thomas is farming and he wants to leave and do something else. You work with your father in a good business in town—and you want to farm. Life gets terribly mixed up at times," Angela sighed.

"And you? What do you want?" asked Thane.

"I—I want you both to be happy," replied Angela.

"But for you?" prompted Thane. "What do you want to do?"

"Oh, I don't know," sighed Angela as tears formed in the corners of her eyes. "For now—I guess I just want to care for the young-sters—to raise them as Mama would have. And I can't. It's too big a job for me, Thane."

"You're doing just fine," he assured her, pressing her hand lightly. "But they won't need you forever. Don't you think you have the right to make some plans of your own?"

"I don't know," said Angela. "I try not to think ahead any further than to getting the children raised." [87–88]

God's plans are better than our dreams.

For I know the thoughts that I think toward you, saith the Lord, thoughts of peace, and not of evil, to give you an expected end.   JEREMIAH 29:11

MIXED MOTIVES

Angela's pulse raced. No young man had ever asked if he could come calling. At last she responded. "It hardly seems the proper time to be calling—when—your father is so—so ill."

"I meant later. After he is—well again."

Carter didn't seem at all embarrassed that he had suggested calling when his father lay desperately ill, and Angela did not believe that he expected his father ever to be well again. A shiver passed through her. She didn't think she cared much for the man, after all. Angela was about to take her leave when she remembered her mama. Mama would never have allowed a child of hers to respond to poor taste with poor taste. *Perhaps his city ways are different than ours,* she reminded herself. *And he has never really known his father.* She turned back to the young man. "It is proper to attend the house of the Lord on any occasion," she said quietly. "And it would be in order for the neighbors to invite a visitor home for dinner following."

"Next Sunday?" he asked, picking up on her clue.

"Next Sunday," she nodded. "The family will be expecting you."

Angela's cheeks burned as she walked home. What had come over her? She had acted just like Trudie with Thomas. She had not appreciated it in Trudie and she did not appreciate it in herself.   [96–97]

*Impure motives on our part can't keep God
from working in someone else's heart.*

For it is God which worketh in you both to will and to do of *his*
good pleasure.   PHILIPPIANS 2:13

TOO LATE

Dinner went well. Thomas was courteous to their guest and spoke with him easily. Angela learned about the young man from listening to their conversation.

He had been raised in Atlanta, his mother's hometown. He had no aunts and uncles, but he did have grandparents. It sounded to Angela as if they doted on the boy.

"How did they feel about your coming west?" asked Thomas.

"They weren't very happy."

"Then why did you come?"

"I had to. I had heard so many little remarks about my father over the years that I had to come and see for myself if he—if he was as they described him."

"And is he?"

"I don't know. I have been trying to piece things together. I think that many things might be accurate. But—I may never know. I still don't really know the man."

Angela felt it was a shame that his coming had been delayed until it was too late for both of them. [103]

It is a shame that some folks never meet their earthly fathers before they die, but it is worse that some don't meet their heavenly father until after they die.

For yet a little while, and he that shall come will come, and will not tarry.   HEBREWS 10:37

THE UNLOVEABLE

Trudie was the first one out to meet them when they arrived. She bounded toward them, her lavender skirts swishing over the grass. She tossed her mane of red hair and gave Thomas a coy look to see if he had taken notice of her. He was busy tethering the horses.

"He hasn't arrived yet," Trudie whispered to Angela, "but Hazel says he promised to come."

Why should Hazel care? wondered Angela. *She is about to be married.*

Trudie opened her mouth to speak again when Angela noticed Roberta. She was in her own special chair—one from which she could not fall. Angela moved toward the girl to speak to her. Trudie trailed along behind until she realized Angela's intentions.

"What if he comes?" she whispered frantically. "He'll catch you talking with her."

Angela gave Trudie a long look and moved on toward the handicapped girl.

[112]

If we cannot love the unloveable
we will never experience love ourselves.

Blessed *is* he that considereth the poor: the Lord will deliver him in time of trouble. . . . Defend the poor and fatherless: do justice to the afflicted and needy.

PSALM 41:1; 82:3

131

Thomas lifted his head.

"Oh, Thomas," admitted Angela. "I never once tried to share my faith with Mr. Stratton."

"Pa tried," responded Thomas. "More than once. I was with him one time. I remember. Pa said that the caring for the state of one's soul was the most important job a man had to do in life. Then he invited Mr. Stratton to church. The man cursed at Pa. I will never forget it. It shocked me that a man would speak in such a way. Then he clenched his fist and shook it in Pa's face. Pa never even blinked. I was hoping Pa would punch him." Thomas stopped to smile momentarily at the memory, then went on.

"Pa didn't back down, but he allowed the man some self-respect—even though he knew he was wrong. 'Mr. Stratton,' he said. 'A man's got a right to make his own decisions in life. I'll grant you that. But I'll also continue to pray for you—and if you ever want to discuss the matter—well, you've got a neighbor and friend just over the fence.' I was so proud of my pa that day," declared Thomas. "I knew right then that it took a bigger man to extend his hand than it did to fight." [117]

We can't push people into heaven but we may be able to lead them to it if we live as if we're already citizens there.

Having your conversation honest among the Gentiles: that . . . they may by *your* good works, which they shall behold, glorify God . . .

1 PETER 2:12

132

Reverend Merrifield spoke to those who, unlike the deceased Mr. Stratton, still had opportunity to prepare to meet God. "Friends," he began, "Christ has gone to prepare a place for us—for each one of us. But for us to take advantage of His goodness—we must prepare our hearts for the place. Have you considered what you must do? Christ will keep His word. The place will be prepared and waiting. It will be ready when you depart this world—if you make preparations. God has told us what we must do to prepare. 'Believe on the Lord Jesus Christ and thou shalt be saved.' Repent—turn from your wickedness and unto God. Ask God to forgive those wrongs—those sins of the past—and to give you a clean heart—clean thoughts, clean actions—so that you might be prepared for the place He has prepared. Accept the forgiveness God provided through the death of His Son."

Angela looked at the crowd of neighbors around the graveside. How many of them might need to hear the words being spoken? Had she really been concerned about their eternal destinies—or had she been too busy caring for her family? Mama would have found the time. *I must be careful so I don't get too taken up with duties that I forget people,* Angela reminded herself. [118–119]

> *If tasks are not done, no one will remember;*
> *if people are not won, God will not forget.*

Then the twelve . . . said, It is not reason that we should leave the word of God, and serve tables.

ACTS 6:2

133

ACTING OR BECOMING

Carter is coming again on Friday night," Angela announced.

Thomas looked up, his eyes filled with surprise.

"I was wondering—could we—could we have a fire in the parlor? That way—should the rest of you like—to read—or whatever—in the kitchen, we won't be in one another's way." There! She had stated her case clearly enough. She was being courted. She needed a bit of privacy. She fixed her eyes on Thomas, her blood pounding through her veins.

Thomas stood quietly, just looking at her; then he reached a hand to the chair in front of him and pushed it back against the table. At last he spoke. "Is this what you want?"

"Why, yes. I—I guess it is."

"You're sure that he shares your faith?"

"He goes to our church—almost every Sunday."

"Angela—it is more than going to church on Sunday. You know that." [122–123]

We can learn to act like a Christian by going to church,
but we can become a Christian only by going to Christ.

Even the righteousness of God *which is* by faith of Jesus Christ unto all and upon all them that believe.

ROMANS 3:22

Carter did call on Friday night. Thane did not. Angela missed seeing him, but quickly pushed all thoughts of him from her mind and gave her full attention to Carter.

Thomas started the fire in the parlor fireplace as Angela had requested and he also must have told the children that Angela was not to be disturbed, for no one came near the parlor door.

Angela prodded Carter gently with leading questions, hoping that he would disclose his beliefs about God. But either he did not understand her meaning or was skillful in evasion, for she never did get a satisfactory answer.

[124]

If we are God's child
God's character will be evident in us.

He that believeth on the Son of God hath the witness in himself: he that believeth not God hath made him a liar; because he believeth not the record that God gave of his Son. And this is the record, that God hath given to us eternal life, and this life is in his Son. He that hath the Son hath life; *and* he that hath not the Son of God hath not life.

1 JOHN 5:10–12

$\mathbf{A}$fter his third cup of coffee, Carter withdrew his pocket watch. "My word!" he exclaimed. "Where have the hours gone? You see the effect you have on me, Angela. I lose all track of time and place."

"It has gone quickly, but we had much to talk about," Angela said.

"Yes," agreed Carter, his eyes serious as they studied her. "We have had. And so much more that we haven't yet discussed. I'm afraid I will have to insist that you allow me more of your time, sweet Angela." His eyes and voice were teasing again. Angela felt that she knew better how to respond when he was in a light mood.

"Well—maybe just a teeny, weeny bit," she said.

"And when might that teeny, weeny bit be available?" he asked. "Could I take you to dinner on Sunday—somewhere? Where does one go for a fancy dinner around here?"

"One does not go for a fancy dinner around here," Angela laughed. "One could get a beef and potato meal at the hotel. But not on Sunday. And not me. I always prepare a special dinner for the family on Sunday."

"See!" he pointed out. "It's like I said. You are always more concerned about others than you are about yourself." [125–126]

If everyone's first concern is self, we all have only one person to rely on. If everyone's first concern is others, we all have many people to rely on.

Look not every man on his own things, but every man also on the things of others.

PHILIPPIANS 2:4

Angela crossed to the stove, brought back the bowls of porridge for her and her younger sister, and settled herself at the table. The others had finished. "You may all be excused," Angela said.

"But we haven't had our Bible story," objected Sara. Angela looked at Thomas who sat, Bible in hand.

"So we haven't," she admitted, a flush touching her cheeks. Then the look turned to one of beseeching. "We are late," she said simply. "Perhaps this once you could read while we eat."

Thomas nodded and began the morning reading. By the time he was ready for prayer, Angela and Louise had finished their porridge and were sitting with hands neatly folded in their laps. They prayed together.

After the door had closed on the four family members, Angela dropped back into a kitchen chair, coffee cup before her.

What will Carter think of all of this? was her first thought. *Well, he did ask me to marry him. I didn't just dream it,* she reminded herself, and then another thought quickly followed. *It's going to be so—so wonderful to have someone to share the responsibility of caring for the family. I know I have always had Thomas—but he can go now—go away to do the work he has always dreamed of. He will be so happy.*   [147–148]

> It is good to try to make others happy,
> but it is best to try to make God happy.

For God shall bring every work into judgment, with every secret thing, whether *it be* good or whether *it be* evil.

ECCLESIASTES 12:14

137

But I thought you said you won."

"I did. I did," said Charlie. "They gave me the deed—and I looked young Mr. Stratton straight in the eye an' told 'im thet he could have his land fer all I cared—an' I handed thet deed right back to 'im."

"But if you didn't care about the land, why did you go to court?" asked Thomas incredulously.

"I weren't gonna be pushed around by some young city-slicker," he sputtered. "The land was mine. It was given to me by the owner."

"But court cases cost—"

"Didn't cost me," said Charlie. "Cost 'im. He had to pay the court costs. An' he got hisself laughed at too. He spent all thet money, and I won the case. Iffen he'd asked face-to-face like a man in the first place, I'd a give it to 'im, but bein' ordered around by a bunch of papers don't sit well with me."

Angela felt anger toward both men. Carter was wrong to try to muscle his way with Charlie. But Charlie was equally wrong to let the whole mess go to court just to prove his silly point. They had both acted like spoiled children. She turned and headed for the stairway, but stopped mid-stride, realizing she was just as foolish. *Never return evil for evil,* she heard the words clearly in her memory.   [159–160]

> *We cannot expect to get mercy for ourselves*
> *if all we want is justice for everyone else.*

Recompense to no man evil for evil.

ROMANS 12:17

KEEPING PROMISES

Would you like me to look for an extra housekeeper for here—for the children—while I am in the city?"

"Oh, but the children won't be staying here," Angela said, wondering why it was necessary to explain this to Carter. "They'll be with me."

"But my dear, I plan to take you to live with me."

Angela nodded. "Of course."

Carter seemed to catch on at last. "You mean," he said slowly, "that you propose to bring all of them along with you to my house?"

Angela nodded, her stomach beginning to churn. She realized he really had meant to leave the youngsters here on their own.

"How you tease," he laughed, giving her a playful shake.

"I am not one to tease about such serious matters." She looked directly into his eyes and saw her own image reflected in them. Her blue eyes held his steadily, and her small frame did not flinch.

"You can't be serious!" he finally exclaimed.

"They go—or I stay," stated Angela simply. "I haven't been much of a mother—but I am the only mother they have. I will not leave them until they have been properly raised." [161–162]

> *The selfish desire we satisfy when we break a promise*
> *will never be worth as much as the self-respect*
> *we gain when we keep one.*

Lord, who shall abide in thy tabernacle? who shall dwell in thy holy hill? . . . *He that* sweareth to *his own* hurt, and changeth not. PSALM 15:1, 4

Carter shifted again. "I can't believe you," he said at last, his eyes narrowing. Then he smiled, but not his sweet, charming smile. "I'm afraid, my dear, that you are all set to be an old maid. No man will marry a woman who brings along three younger siblings—even if she is pleasing to the eyes."

Angela swallowed hard and nodded. "Then so be it," she replied with all the courage she could muster. She moved to get his hat and coat and handed them to him without a word.

He looked at her, anger filling his eyes, and then he began to laugh, a coarse, bitter laugh that made Angela shiver. She felt as though she had been struck, but still she did not flinch.

"Good night, my dear," he said.

"Goodbye, Mr. Stratton," she replied and turned back to the fire until she heard him leave the room. [162]

When people don't get what they want
we find out what kind of people they are.

The desire of the righteous *is* only good: *but* the expectation of the wicked *is* wrath. . . . The heart of the righteous studieth to answer: but the mouth of the wicked poureth out evil things.   PROVERBS 11:23; 15:28

CHARACTER

Not until Angela was in the privacy of her own bedroom did she allow the tears to flow. She didn't bother to remove her clothes before throwing herself onto her bed and letting the sobs shake her slender body.

"He's right," she cried into her pillow. "He's right. I will be an old maid. No one will ever, ever marry me with three others to care for. I know it. I know it."

Angela cried long and hard, but in the end she wiped her tears and resolutely got up to prepare for bed.

"I don't care," she told her image in the mirror. "I am quite ready to be an old maid. I made Mama a promise—and with God's help I will keep it. I will raise them. I will. I will. And I will never—never look at another man again. How could I have been so foolish? Why did I say yes so quickly? Mama taught me more sense than that. Thomas was right. I never really knew Carter. I did not realize the kind of person he really is. I am just so thankful—so thankful—that I found out in time to prevent a—a tragic mistake." [162–163]

We cannot know if a person has good character
until we see how he or she responds in bad circumstances.

The tree is known by *his* fruit . . . out of the abundance of the heart the mouth speaketh.

Matthew 12:33–34

SELF-SACRIFICE

Angela lifted her head and took a deep breath. "There won't be a wedding, after all," she said matter-of-factly.

"He backed out?" Thomas asked through clenched teeth.

"Let's just say we changed our minds," Angela hurried on.

Thomas reached for her hand. "Are you terribly disappointed?"

"I honestly don't know," she managed to say. "In some ways—yes. But I—I've done some praying and—well, I think it's best this way. I don't think Carter and I were—well—right for each other. But I'm awfully sorry about you—"

"About me?" cut in Thomas. "What do you mean?"

"Well, you could have left the farm. Gone to do your work with seed like you've always dreamed. I know how much it means to you," she rushed on, "and as long as you need to be here—for the children and me—I know you won't just leave us and go," said Angela with a little shrug.

"You mean you thought—" Thomas leaned toward his sister and spoke softly but firmly, "Angela, don't you ever marry anyone to try to make things better for the rest of the family." [167–168]

We can do more harm than good when
we put the needs of others above obedience to God.

Martha was cumbered about much serving. . . . And Jesus . . . said unto her, Martha, Martha, thou art careful and troubled about many things: But one thing is needful: and Mary hath chosen that good part.

LUKE 10:40–42

STRENGTH TO RISE

Carter is letting me choose my own attendant," Trudie announced, "and I picked you."

Angela felt the blood draining from her face. "Oh, but I—"

"Don't try to say no. You are my best friend. I've already told Carter. He says he'd love to have you share our happy moment. He was so sweet about it. He will even shop for a dress for you. He insists—he says he'll pick one just for you." Trudie babbled on. "And he said he would look after everything. And, oh—you should see the house! Carter has had it completely redone. It's gorgeous! And I am to have help—in the kitchen and with the cleaning. Not Gus, of course. Gus has been dismissed. There's a new cook coming from the city. Carter says he is sick and tired of flapjacks and fried bacon." Trudie stopped to laugh as though the comment had been witty or cute.

Trudie went on and on about the wedding, about the house, about Carter. Angela tried to listen but her thoughts kept wandering. She continued to knead the dough, giving it such a thorough rolling and pounding that she wasn't sure it would have the strength to rise. [186–187]

After a thorough pounding by forces outside us, only the
power of God inside us can give us the strength to rise.

He giveth power to the faint; and to *them that have* no might he increaseth strength.

ISAIAH 40:29

I've been doin' some thinkin'," said Charlie.

He was silent so Angela prompted. "About?"

"About yer ma and pa. Their religion. What they used to say. You know what?"

"What?" asked Angela.

"I even been tryin' to live like they did." He straightened his shoulders and looked directly into her eyes. Then he seemed to sag.

"Guess I don't know enough about it—'cause I keep gettin' all tripped up. Just when I think I got the hang of behavin' proper, I go an' do somethin' all wrong. Don't know how your folks kept all those rules straight."

"You think that their—their faith was a bunch of rules?" asked Angela softly.

"Wasn't it?"

"No. No—it wasn't rules," explained Angela hesitantly. "It starts with the heart." [189–190]

Following rules of proper behavior won't lead us to God,
but following God will lead to proper behavior.

But in vain they do worship me, teaching for doctrines the commandments of men.

MATTHEW 15:9

A NEW HEART

Angela placed her hand over her heart. "We are all sinners. We can't be good enough to earn our way into heaven—none of us. God knew that. That's why He sent His Son Jesus to pay the penalty for sin. He said that the wages for sin was death. That part He didn't change. But instead of making each one of us die for our own misdeeds, He allowed Jesus to die for all of us. But even though the penalty has been paid, it's of no effect unless we accept it. It's like getting a present that you don't accept. You have to accept it like a gift—with thankfulness."

Charlie was silent while he pondered the words.

"That's all?" he asked at last.

"Well, not quite. I mean, when we admit we're sinners, then we ask for His forgiveness and accept His gift—like I said. Then He does the rest. He cleanses us. The Bible says He gives us a new heart—a clean heart." [190–191]

God takes from us the bad that we can't get rid of
and gives to us the good that we can't acquire.

A new heart also will I give you, and a new spirit will I put within you: and I will take away the stony heart out of your flesh, and I will give you an heart of flesh.

EZEKIEL 36:26

BLAME

Thane had sent word with Thomas that he would come calling on Friday night if it was convenient for Angela. She would not have dreamed of turning him down. After all her years of close friendship with Thane, Angela felt strangely nervous and excited.

Stop it, she scolded herself, lifting a trembling hand to brush her hair back into a neat knot. But she could not control her feelings. She had never been this agitated when Carter was calling.

Carter! With his name came the painful memory of his curling lips and final cutting warning: "You are all set to be an old maid. No man will marry a woman who brings along three younger siblings."

The words brought Angela's hands to a halt. She clutched at the combs she was about to place in her hair. Carter was right. No man—not even Thane—should be expected to take on a ready-made family. Angela leaned against the bureau and shut her eyes tightly, but the tears squeezed out from under the lids.

"It wouldn't be fair. It wouldn't be fair," her heart cried. "Oh, God, if only Mama——" But Angela checked her thoughts. For the first time in her life she had been about to blame her mama for not staying with them. [203]

It is unwise to place blame for our circumstances, because what seems bad in light of what we know today may be good in light of what we find out tomorrow.

Lord, if thou hadst been here, my brother had not died.

JOHN 11:32

146

LOVE UNLIMITED

The two walked in silence for a few minutes, then Thane started the conversation. "My mama always said that a girl is old enough to know her own mind at nineteen." His voice held a teasing note.

"You have a very wise mama," responded Angela.

Thane stopped and drew Angela close beside him. "Then if you know your mind," he began, his voice serious, "are you ready to promise to be my wife?"

Angela's world began to spin. She caught her breath and strained in the semidarkness to study his face. He was not teasing. "Do you mean—?" she began. She should have explained to Thane that she could not leave the children until her task was completed.

"I—I can't!" she cried, a sob catching in her throat. She saw in the moonlight the surprised and hurt look that crossed Thane's face. "I promised Mama that I'd—that I'd care for the family—"

"You can still care for the family," he interrupted.

"But—but you won't want to—to take on a whole family when you wed," she sobbed and leaned against him to cry.

"Angela, when I asked you to marry me, I knew that you'd never leave them. I have always known that it would mean caring for the family." [210–211]

No promise of love is true unless it includes all of you.

Charity . . . beareth all things, believeth all things, hopeth all things, endureth all things.

1 CORINTHIANS 13:4, 7

Y ou gave me the scare of my life when you were seeing Carter," Thane said solemnly. He drew her into his arms. She could hear the beating of his heart as she lay her ear against his chest.

"It would have been all wrong," she whispered.

"I know," he answered. "I'm so thankful to God that you realized it before it was too late. I have never prayed so hard in all my life."

Angela closed her eyes tightly and breathed a prayer of her own.

"I'm still waiting for my answer," he whispered into her hair.

"Oh, Thane," she responded, looking up at him. "I don't think it's fair to you. It won't be easy. You have no idea just how hard—"

Thane's arms tightened around her. "Angela, just answer me."

"Yes—yes, I'd be happy to be your wife."

Thane kissed her then while a million twinkling stars clapped their hands above them. The moon dipped thoughtfully behind a cloud, allowing them a few moments of total privacy. When the glow of moonlight restored light to the world around them, Thane spoke. "Would you like to go in? We have a lot of plans to make."

Angela agreed. Her heart was singing. Her world was spinning in a flood of glorious light and color. She lifted her face to the open sky. "Oh, God," she breathed. "I'm so happy. Tell Mama, will you, Father? I want so much to share this moment with her." [211]

A celebration is incomplete
if those we love cannot share our joy.

The flowers appear on the earth; the time of the singing *of birds* is come.   SOLOMON 2:12

FOLLOWING THE BOOK

Been readin' yer ma's Bible," Charlie announced. "Understand a lot of things I didn't understand before. Gus an' me figure it's about time we got ourselves straightened out and attendin' church. As soon as it warms up we figure we'll have the preacher baptize us in the crick."

"Oh—but first," began Angela, "first you must make your—your commitment—to the faith."

"Did thet," said Charlie simply.

Gus nodded. "Yep. Yep. Did thet."

"You did?" said Angela, her eyes opening wider. "But how did you know—I mean, what did you—"

"Jest followed the Book," said Charlie. "Yer mama had all the places marked—jest like ya said. We jest followed the Book."

"Jest followed the Book," parroted Gus.

"It works," continued Charlie. "I got thet new heart—right in here." He placed a calloused hand over his shirt front. "Feel changed. New. Just like the Book says."

"Yup," put in Gus. "Changed—jest like the Books says."

"I—I don't know what to say," Angela stammered. "I'm so happy. Papa and Mama would both be so pleased." [216–217]

The best way to lead people to God
is to "follow the Book" ourselves.

Joy shall be in heaven over one sinner that repenteth, more than over ninety and nine just persons, which need no repentance.   LUKE 15:7

149

BECOMING ONE

Thomas lifted the family Bible and was about to begin the morning reading when Louise interrupted.

"Couldn't we play the game? Just once more? Please. It won't take us long. Please."

"But we can still play the game. Just as often as we like," said Angela. "Thane is always happy to play it with us."

"But Thomas will be gone," said Louise, fighting hard to keep back the tears. "It just won't be the same anymore."

No. It would not be the same. Thomas would be gone—leaving to pursue his dream of schooling and research just as soon as she and Thane returned from their short wedding trip. And then Derek would be leaving them to make his way in the world. And before they all turned around, Louise would be grown—then little Sara.

Before Angela could start crying, a new thought came to her. She would always have Thane. There would be no day when he would grow up and leave her. That was the marvel of God's great plan. Through good times and bad, through sickness and health, in weakness and in strength, Thane would be with her as long as God granted them years on earth. She lifted her head, her eyes shining in appreciation for the wisdom and love of her Father. [218–219]

Only God's wisdom could conceive of a plan
that would for life join a woman and a man.

Wherefore they are no more twain, but one flesh. What therefore God hath joined together, let not man put asunder.

MATTHEW 19:6

NEW BEGINNINGS

Thomas started the memories. "I remember the morning I was baptized. Mama took me in her arms and told me she was proud of me for making the right decision—then she looked me in the eyes and said, 'Thomas—always be true to the step you are taking. Don't ever—ever think of turning back.'"

Angela noted that somewhere along the way they had changed from recalling memories to also remembering the lessons Mama so subtly taught with each little incident of childhood.

Derek cleared his throat. "I remember one morning when I went out to feed the chickens and the mother cat was running across the yard with a little dead bird. I chased her and got it back and brought it in to Mama. I was crying and she just hugged me for a long time and let me cry and then she said, 'Son, don't fight death. Death is a part of life. One thing dies that another might live. God is a wise God. He has a purpose for all things—even death. And for us—His special creation—death is the only gate to eternal life. When the time comes for me to join Him, though I might wish to linger a bit, it will be a triumphant time. Remember that.'" [219–220]

With God, nothing good ever ends;
even death is the start of something better.

Though our outward man perish, yet the inward *man* is renewed day by day.

2 CORINTHIANS 4:16

REWARD

Angela looked around the table at her family members and cleared her throat. "I remember," she began with trembling voice, "when I was about ten years old, Mama was sick in bed and I was sent to the field to take lunch to Papa. On the way home I found some early roses. They were the first ones I had seen that spring— just beginning to open—bright and pink and sweet-smelling. I knew how much Mama loved the spring roses so I stopped to pick some. Just a little handful. That's all there were. Then I continued on home, thinking how happy Mama would be. I had to cross the creek and it was higher than usual. Papa had thrown a log across it, but I wasn't very good at walking the log. I was about halfway across when I started to lose my balance. I grabbed for an overhanging limb and managed to keep myself from falling in. But I dropped the roses. I stood there crying as I watched the stream carry them off. When I got home I was still crying. I went into Mama's bedroom and threw myself against her bed and told her what had happened.

"She put her arms around me and pulled me close. 'Angela,' she said, 'you are my flowers. My roses. You and your brothers and sisters. You make up my bouquet. And a more lovely bouquet never graced the home of any woman. I will always see you as my beautiful, beautiful roses. I don't need any others.'" [221–222]

> God's beauty is most evident
> in a blooming flower and a budding life.
>
> Children *are* an heritage of the Lord . . .
>
> PSALM 127:3

153

A Woman Named Damaris

MONEY

One glance at her father told Damaris that he had spent a good deal of his afternoon at the saloon.

"Get in here, girl!" roared her father. "Give yer poor ma a hand. Don't ya care a'tall thet she's got all the work to do?" The man shook his head and began to curse before ending his tirade.

"Yes, Pa," Damaris whispered. No point telling him that already she had drawn water for the two cows. That she had hoed the garden in the hot morning sun. That she had walked into town with the eggs and traded them for salt and flour. That she had chopped the wood for the fire and hauled the water to replenish the kitchen buckets. Or that Mama herself had given her permission to rest a few minutes. To answer back would get her the back of his hand or a thrashing if he felt so inclined.

He sat at the table mumbling his complaints and curses as Damaris and her mother scurried about to prepare him a hot meal. They did not speak or even look at each other. They did not need to; they had played this scene before—many times—whenever there was money. Damaris hated money. Hated what it did to her pa. To her mama. And she hated the fear coursing through her now, shriveling her body into a quaking, trembling mass. [12]

Money is not inherently evil. Its virtue depends on the character of the person using it.

For the love of money is the root of all evil: which while some coveted after, they have erred from the faith.

1 TIMOTHY 6:10

CHOICES

It was a pleasure for Damaris to be sitting serenely at the table with her mama, knowing that it would be hours before her pa could be of any threat to them again.

"Were you reading?" her mama asked.

Damaris nodded, seeing in her mama's eyes complete understanding. She wondered how her mama knew, how they could communicate so completely with so few words.

They sipped coffee in silence for a few minutes, then Mrs. Withers spoke again. "You have pretty eyes," she said. "They are just like my papa's. He had dark brown eyes too. I took after Mama. My eyes are gray. I was always disappointed about that. Wanted dark eyes like my pa. One hasn't much choice about eyes, I guess," the woman mused aloud. "Shouldn't even waste time thinkin' 'bout it." She stirred her coffee, then took a deep breath and said, "One should be more concerned with things thet can be changed. Who we are—what we become—how our lives affect others." [15–16]

It is difficult to choose what's right
if all we ever see is what's wrong.

He will eat curds and honey when he knows enough to reject
the wrong and choose the right.

ISAIAH 7:15 (NIV)

ALTERNATIVES

Damaris looked directly at her mama. The thin, pale woman sitting opposite her had slightly graying hair that was pushed haphazardly in a bun at the base of her neck. It had become dislodged in the struggle with her pa and several strands of shorter hair curled in wisps against her shallow cheeks. The longer strands had been tucked recklessly behind her ears. For the first time in her young life, Damaris wondered who her mama really was, and who she had been before she met and married her pa. Would life have been different if she had married someone else? Never married at all?

Damaris had never thought to ask such questions. She had accepted their life together as the way things were. Now she found herself wondering if there were alternatives. Could life have been different? For Mama? Even for her?

[16]

*The choices we make today determine
the alternatives we'll have tomorrow.*

Choose you this day whom ye will serve; whether the gods which your fathers served that *were* on the other side of the flood, or the gods of the Amorites, in whose land ye dwell: but as for me and my house, we will serve the Lord.

JOSHUA 24:15

159

Long into the night Damaris lay thinking. If only there was no money. If only her pa didn't make the trips into town to spend his time at the saloon tables. If only her mama didn't look so old and tired all of the time. If only—

Damaris checked herself. There was no use going on. Things were as they were. Nothing would change. Damaris touched the scar above her temple. At least her pa had not thrown anything at her—this time. He had not slapped her nor twisted her arm. They had gotten off easy this time—both her and her mama. But what about next time? And the time after that? She lived in fear and dread of each new day, and she was sure her mama did likewise.

What if her pa awoke and found out that they had been drinking his precious coffee? What if he discovered that an expensive-looking brooch had been hidden from him for many years? What if he learned of the watch? Damaris slipped a hand under the pillow to feel the items. For a moment she felt a flash of anger toward her mama. Why had she given her these dangerous possessions? [19–20]

When we can't change the way things are
we need to consider what God wants us to do
to change the way things will be.

In the morning thou shalt say, Would God it were even! and at even thou shalt say, Would God it were morning! for the fear of thine heart wherewith thou shalt fear, and for the sight of thine eyes which thou shalt see.

DEUTERONOMY 28:67

LEARNING

Damaris puzzled again over her mother's words. *Many girls of seventeen are on their own. You could pass for seventeen.* The strange message played and replayed through the young girl's mind. But she could make no sense of it.

There are choices we can make, the voice went on. Choices? What choices. Not the color of one's eyes. Mama had made that clear enough. Then what choices? Damaris had never had choices. If she could have chosen, she would be attending school like all of the other children in the neighborhood. But she couldn't choose. Her pa had done that for her when she reached the age of twelve.

"Ain't right fer you to be fritterin' away yer day when yer ma is home doin' all the chores," he had growled. "Girl big as you should be able to earn her keep."

So Damaris had been taken from school and put to work with the household and farm chores. It wasn't that she minded the work, but she did hate to miss the classes. Now she had no access to books. Books and the adventure of learning. [20]

*We will never stop learning
unless we lose the will to learn.*

A wise *man* will hear, and will increase learning; and a man
of understanding shall attain unto wise counsels.

PROVERBS 1:5

161

Damaris urged herself up the stairs to the loft and quietly gathered her few belongings into her shawl. Then she stepped onto her bed, up onto the dresser, and carefully lifted aside the trapdoor.

From the safety of the rafters she withdrew her pieces of bread and her cloth-wrapped treasures. With one final look around the dusty cavern, Damaris eased herself back through the trapdoor, pulled the cover into place, and stepped to the bed, then to the floor. With as little noise as possible she bound everything together. Then she crept from the room without looking back. As she passed the bedroom where her mother lay, she hesitated for one moment, listened to the silence, then sighed deeply and continued on tiptoe.

The kitchen door closed softly behind her. She had made a choice and taken the first step on her own. She only wished with all of her heart that her mama was going with her. Her heart pounded with the enormity of her daring. She had no idea what lay before her, nor how she would ever make her way in the unknown world she was facing. But at least now she was free to make her own choices. [26]

With the freedom to make our own choices
comes the responsibility to make the right ones.

I call heaven and earth to record this day against you, *that* I have set before you life and death, blessing and cursing: therefore choose life, that both thou and thy seed may live.

DEUTERONOMY 30:19

LOOKING AHEAD

It was getting dark before Damaris realized she had gone about as far as she could for the first day. She had no idea how far she had traveled, and the road seemed to be petering out. She wondered if she would soon come to some impassable obstacle. Damaris made her way toward the side of the road, looking about to find some kind of shelter.

She eased herself onto a stump by the roadside and drew out her bottle. Two wee sips were all she allowed her parched throat. Then she unwrapped the little store of bread and lifted out one piece. It wasn't nearly enough to ease her hunger, but Damaris's hunger had gone unsatisfied on more than one occasion so she was set to suffer a grumbling stomach now.

Finding a large tree with a canopy of spreading branches, she pushed her way close to the trunk. Then she put down her shawl-wrapped bundle for a pillow, tucked her worn blanket closely about her, and eased herself to the ground. Damaris kicked her burning feet free of the blanket and extended them into the cool of the evening air. She did not waste time lamenting. Did not even allow herself to wonder "What if . . . ?" She would need all her energy for the ordeal ahead.   [28–29]

We cannot decide the right way to go
by looking only at where we have been.

And Jesus said unto him, No man, having put his hand to the
plough, and looking back, is fit for the kingdom of God.

LUKE 9:62

163

DILIGENCE

Mr. Brown led Damaris to a covered wagon somewhat apart from the others. He lifted the canvas flap and called, "Martha."

A woman holding a crying baby emerged.

"This here young girl wants to travel west. Says she'll work in exchange for the ride. Ya interested?"

The woman studied Damaris. There were questions in her eyes but she did not voice them. At length she nodded. She already looked tired and the trip had not yet begun. "You'll ride in the second wagon," she informed Damaris. "Our oldest boy is drivin' and there are three more young'uns in there. It'll be yer job to care fer'em when we are on the move. When we stop ya can busy yerself with helpin' get the meals an' sech. Put yer things in the wagon there an' gather some wood fer a fire. We'll need to eat before we set off, an' we don't have long to be fixin' it."

Damaris nodded. She moved toward the wagon indicated and hoisted her small bundle of possessions under the canvas. Then she made her way to the small grove of trees beside the road. She would hasten to carry out her first assignment lest the woman change her mind and leave her behind. [48]

There are many ways to acquire money but only through diligence and hard work can we gain true riches.

He becometh poor that dealeth *with* a slack hand: but the hand of the diligent maketh rich.

PROVERBS 10:4

COMFORT

It was a simple meal that Damaris prepared but no one complained, and after she had washed up the dishes and packed them away for the trip she saw a look of relief on the woman's face.

"I need to nurse this one," the woman said, lifting the baby and rising from the stool where she sat. "Thet one needs a nap iffen ya can coax him to settle," and she nodded her head at the boy who had been crying and hanging on to his mother's skirts ever since Damaris first saw him.

Damaris had misgivings as she picked up the young tot and headed for the wagon she had been told was hers to share. He screamed for his mother, but Damaris continued walking.

She knew very little about caring for children, having had no siblings of her own. Reason told her, however, that if the child was to be settled for a nap, he first had to be comforted, so when she reached the wagon she crawled aboard and began to gently rock the little one in her arms, singing a song that her mama used to sing to her. [49]

We are to comfort others because
we ourselves have been comforted.

Who comforteth us in all our tribulation, that we may be able to comfort them which are in any trouble, by the comfort wherewith we ourselves are comforted of God.

2 CORINTHIANS 1:4

165

For the first few days of the journey Damaris was terrified that the captain would discover her and send her back to the town where she had joined the wagon train.

About the third day he finally saw her, but he said nothing, just scowled, nodded, then passed her by. Damaris breathed a relieved sigh. She was safe. She could continue her trip west.

Still, Damaris chose to stay well out of his way, not wishing to bother him or cross him.

One thing about the journey pleased Damaris. There were no towns—and no saloons. Never once on the whole trail did Damaris see a drunken man. Never once did she see a woman or child bearing cuts or bruises because of someone's fit of drunken rage. Damaris, as eager as she was to reach a town, also dreaded the thought, sure that once they arrived the men would return to their normal way of life. [54]

If we don't fear God we have
good reason to dread the future.

"The Lord is my helper; I will not be afraid. What can man do to me?"   HEBREWS 13:6

166

NEW LIFE

Three days! Only three more days. It sounded like a release from a moving prison. The whole camp was abuzz that evening. Damaris even heard some singing.

Damaris was too excited to sleep well that night. The flap of the wagon had been turned back to allow a little cool air to enter, and through the opening she could see the moon hanging silvery overhead. She could stand it no longer. She eased herself out from under the blankets, slipped her dress over her head, grabbed her shawl, and left the wagon. Edgar did not stir.

The captain's rule was that no one was to stray from the camp, by night or by day. But if they were close to a town Damaris reasoned, there should be no danger. Besides, she would not go far.

She crept past the other wagons and followed the small stream for a short distance. Then she sat down on a large rock by its shore and sighed, taking a deep breath of the clear night air.

In just three more days she would be out West. She would be free to settle in a new town, forget her short but troubled past, and make a new life for herself. [54–55]

Whatever new life we can make for ourselves cannot compare with the new life God has already made for us.

Therefore we are buried with him by baptism into death: that like as Christ was raised up from the dead by the glory of the Father, even so we also should walk in newness of life.

ROMANS 6:4

JUSTICE

Damaris turned and saw the captain standing a scant five feet behind her. She caught her breath, knowing she had broken his rule—his one, unchanging, indisputable order. She had left the train. Alone.

She was sure he would sentence her to immediate and terrible consequences. Should she dart and run or sit meekly and face his wrath? The latter had always worked best in the past. Only once had she tried to dodge under her pa's arm and avoid the punishment he had in mind. The beating she received that time was the worst one of her entire life. She had never tried it again.

Now she sat silently, appearing calm, but quivering inside.

The man moved closer and Damaris steeled herself for the blow that was to come. To her surprise his hand did not raise to strike her. Instead, he lowered himself to a rock a short distance away.

[56]

When those in authority are just,
those under authority are safe.

The God of Israel said, the Rock of Israel spake to me, He that ruleth over men *must be* just, ruling in the fear of God.

2 SAMUEL 23:3

Damaris let out her breath. Not only had he discovered her tonight but apparently had observed her walks in the past. Why hadn't he said something before?

" 'Sides," he said with a glance toward Damaris, "I had my eye on ya."

Damaris gathered the shawl more closely about her. It offered little protection from a beating but it was all she had.

"I decided right from the start thet as long as you stayed close an' caused no harm, I'd allow ya those little pieces of alone time. Couldn't bear to be so shut in like you been all the time. Couldn't bear it."

Damaris could not believe her ears. Did she understand him correctly? Was there to be no punishment? Had he actually allowed her to break his one steadfast rule?   [57]

Those who won't admit wrongdoing
can't receive mercy.

Remember me, O my God, *concerning* this also, and spare
me according to the greatness of thy mercy.

NEHEMIAH 13:22

WRONG ASSUMPTIONS

Damaris dished the porridge and handed Mr. Brown his plate. He was in such a hurry that he didn't seem to mind that it was half-raw. He washed it down with long gulps of weak coffee then stood and glanced at the sky. There was no break in the cloudy curtain. "Get the kids up," he said to Damaris. "I need to take thet wagon to town fer supplies."

Damaris moved to obey but she wondered how she would ever get through the morning with four youngsters out in the rain.

Mr. Brown did not notice her concern. He was adding another item to his long list. As he unfolded his paper, Damaris saw the bills tucked inside it. She drew in her breath with a quick gulp of air. *He has money! And he's headin' to town!* Damaris knew what that meant. They likely wouldn't see him for the rest of the day and when he did appear again—there would be trouble—for all of them. She moved quickly to awaken the children. If Mr. Brown was annoyed when he left he might be even more irritable when he returned after a day at the saloon. [69–70]

> *We can be seriously mistaken when we assume that*
> *all the people we meet are like all the people we know.*

Philip findeth Nathanael, and saith unto him, We have found him, of whom Moses in the law, and the prophets, did write, Jesus of Nazareth, the son of Joseph. And Nathanael said unto him, Can there any good thing come out of Nazareth? Philip saith unto him, Come and see.

JOHN 1:45–46

COMPASSION

The voice behind Damaris brought her quickly to an upright position. The wagon master stood there, his hat droopy with the morning rain, his shoulders seeming to sag under the weight of his wet shirt. "I've brought you a—a letter of reference," he said as he withdrew a folded piece of paper from his shirt pocket. "I don't know iffen you'll need this—but I thought it could do no harm."

Damaris was surprised at his consideration. He had been so kind to her—he who had not wanted her on his wagon train in the first place. "I—I thank you," she fumbled as she accepted the bit of paper.

"I do hope thet all goes well fer you. Brown says he won't leave you stranded. Will try to get ya located in town before he moves on to his homestead," said the man, looking directly into her eyes. "God bless ya."

Damaris had never heard such concern and sincerity in a man's voice. She could not speak, so she just nodded and swallowed hard. Then the captain turned and was gone.   [72]

Acts of compassion do not go unnoticed.

Blessed *be* ye of the Lord; for ye have compassion on me.

1 SAMUEL 23:21

171

PLEASANT WORDS

It was almost noon before Damaris sighted the returning Brown wagon. The girls must have spotted it about the same time, for Damaris heard a clamor from the shelter by the fire.

"It's Pa!" one screeched, and the others soon joined her.

Damaris shifted the sleeping Edgar in her arms. She rocked him gently and pulled the blanket up more closely around his ears. *Now we are in for it—all of us,* thought Damaris. *I hate the thought of it.*

But the girls were dancing under the tree-strung tarp and continuing to yell, "Pa's comin'. Pa's comin'." There didn't seem to be any worry or concern in any of their faces.

And sure enough, when the wagon arrived, Mr. Brown seemed as sober as when he had driven off to town.

The noise got louder and Mr. Brown laughed and rumpled wet hair with a large calloused hand. Finally he pulled a small bag from his pocket and passed it to Bella with instructions to share equally. "An' don't fergit Damaris," he added.

Damaris looked up in surprise. She still had not gotten over the shock of a sober employer—and then to be offered a sweet besides. Damaris could not believe her ears and eyes.   [73–74]

We can never make the world a pleasant place
by using unpleasant words.

Pleasant words *are as* an honeycomb, sweet to the soul, and
health to the bones. PROVERBS 16:24

Mrs. Stacy felt quite good about their accomplishments. "Looks like it will work out just fine," she said with satisfaction. "Mr. MacKenzie will take you a couple of days—part time—an' he'll put your wage on account. You ought to be able to buy some shoes come winter an' maybe even a piece of yard goods. And Miss Dover will take you a couple days—part time. You'll sew for her in exchange for a wage. An' you'll have your board an' room with me in exchange for your help there. That should work out just fine."

Things did work out fine for Mrs. Stacy, but Damaris felt as if she was always on the run. She would just be settled into a task at Mrs. Stacy's when word would come that she was needed at Mr. MacKenzie's store. Or she would be hanging up the broom at the store and Mr. MacKenzie would say, "You can hustle over to Miss Dover's now."

She tried to convince herself that she really didn't mind. That it kept her from boredom. That it acquainted her with the people of the town. That she was young and the exercise did her good. But in spite of all the reasoning she did with herself, Damaris longed for a sense of actually belonging—somewhere. [91–94]

God satisfies every longing of those belonging to Him.

For he satisfieth the longing soul, and filleth the hungry soul
with goodness. PSALM 107:9

KNOWLEDGE OF GOD

It has always bothered me that there is no church here," Miss Dover remarked. "Year after year I have prayed that God would send this town a minister—and I still pray. I believe that someday—perhaps soon—the answer will come. It pains me to see children growing up without any knowledge of God. Why, I never would have gotten through those difficult times had I not had Him. I was so thankful that my mama and my papa had given me a strong base of faith. When I couldn't understand, I could just trust. I knew without a doubt that God loved me—and He wouldn't forsake me."

Damaris had no idea what the woman was talking about. She listened politely, making no comment, but the words were foreign to her. She had heard her mama make references to God. But Damaris had never heard talk about trust—or about God loving people. But then, Miss Dover was an easy person to love. Perhaps God did love her. [99–100]

People cannot trust in a God they do not know.
And they should be able to get to know Him
by being around those who trust Him.

Hear the word of the Lord, ye children of Israel: for the Lord hath a controversy with the inhabitants of the land, because *there is* no truth, nor mercy, nor knowledge of God in the land. . . . My people are destroyed for lack of knowledge.

HOSEA 4:1, 6

LOVELY PEOPLE

Miss Dover was gentle and kind. She dressed simply yet neatly. She spoke words of kindness wherever she went. Men always doffed their hats and women always smiled a good morning, and even children grinned and pressed a little closer when Miss Dover walked the streets. She was to Damaris everything that a true lady should be. Without realizing it, Damaris tried to pattern her own conduct after that of Miss Dover.

The kind woman seemed to genuinely enjoy Damaris's company and expressed interest in all her employee was doing. Damaris could not understand or explain why, but she felt comfortable with Miss Dover—as though a very important part of herself was able to function—to exist—in the presence of the older woman.

So Damaris spent her days rushing through duties at the boardinghouse and the store so she could run breathlessly across the street, slide into a chair beside her mending basket, and enjoy Miss Dover's presence. [106]

People who love God can't help but be lovely people.

The aged women likewise, that *they be* in behaviour as becometh holiness, not false accusers, not given to much wine, teachers of good things.

TITUS 2:3

176

FOOLISHNESS

Damaris still felt a bit uneasy expressing her thoughts, but Miss Dover drew her out little by little.

"I love King David!" Miss Dover exclaimed. "He was so full of life—of feeling—of love," she said, using her plump hand to express the depth of her emotions.

Damaris looked up from her sewing, her eyes wide with wonder. Then, in barely a whisper, said, "But he did some pretty bad things."

Miss Dover smiled. "Ah, yes. He did. But he was so repentant. So deeply troubled by his sin. He cried out to God with such remorse. That is what really counts," said Miss Dover. "Not all the foolish mistakes we make, though we should certainly seek the will of God before we make a move—not after—so that we need not make such terrible mistakes in the first place; but if we do make mistakes, then we must be remorseful. Repentant. We must ask for forgiveness. God will forgive if we confess our sin."

Damaris had never heard such strange talk. [106–107]

Believers should be neither surprised nor offended when unbelievers consider their beliefs foolish.

For the preaching of the cross is to them that perish foolishness; but unto us which are saved it is the power of God. . . . But the natural man receiveth not the things of the Spirit of God: for they are foolishness unto him: neither can he know *them*, because they are spiritually discerned.

1 CORINTHIANS 1:18; 2:14

TOO GOOD TO BE TRUE

Damaris loved many of the characters of the stories, but the man Jesus drew her like no other. He was different from any man she had ever known. She imagined His birth in a cattle shed with no bed but a cow's manger. She exulted as He walked the dusty roads speaking words of peace and healing the sick. She chuckled with glee when He outwitted the proud Pharisees who tried to trick Him with their questions. And she agonized when He was sentenced to death and forced to drag His cross through the streets of the city to Golgotha. When she came at last to the story of the open tomb, Damaris hugged her knees and choked back the words she wished to say out loud. It was all so exciting, so perfect. She had never read a story like it. "I wish He had really lived," she often said to herself. "I wish He had lived right here in Dixen."

Here was a man Damaris felt she could trust. In fact, Damaris could find no reason *not* to trust Him. If only He were real.

[127–128]

When it seems that nothing good is true we rejoice in knowing that the One who is true is good.

But these are written, that ye might believe that Jesus is the Christ, the Son of God; and that believing ye might have life through his name.   JOHN 20:31

SERVING

Suddenly realizing that she should be assuming her chores instead of admiring the new hat Miss Dover had given her, Damaris placed the hat back in its box and turned to Miss Dover.

"What do you wish me to do?" she asked.

"All is done—for the moment," said the woman. "Gil is coming for dinner too. But he won't be here until a bit later."

Damaris panicked. She hadn't realized that she would be asked to serve Gil.

"Why don't you run on home and put on your prettiest dress. The one we made you last summer. You have hardly worn it. If we should clean up together later," Miss Dover went on, "I'll give you a heavy apron to cover it. But I want you to feel ladylike and lovely as my guest."

"Your guest?" Damaris could not stop the words.

"You didn't know you were to be my guest? Why, yes. For Christmas dinner. You and Gil. The two people dearest to me."

Damaris stood still, unable to move or speak. She had never been anyone's dinner guest. She knew how to serve, but she wasn't sure she knew how to be served. [132]

There is no higher calling than that of serving.

And whosoever of you will be the chiefest, shall be servant of all. For even the Son of man came not to be ministered unto, but to minister, and to give his life a ransom for many.

MARK 10:44–45

179

HIDING WHO WE ARE

Damaris could not hide her nervousness as she sat at dinner with Miss Dover and Gil Lewis. Damaris had never shared a festive table with anyone before. She was so conscious of her table manners, or lack of them, that she feared she would break out into a sweat. But Damaris was quick to learn. She had listened closely to all that Miss Dover had said. She watched her hostess carefully, every now and then receiving a smile of encouragement or a nod of approval. Even so, Damaris found it hard to relax and enjoy herself. She wasn't even able to take much part in the conversation. Miss Dover and Gil chatted comfortably. Damaris sensed that they had discussed many issues in the past, and today was simply a matter of catching up on the latest happenings in each other's lives.

They made attempts to bring Damaris into the conversation. When asked a direct question she gave an honest, though short, reply, but she never did relax enough to really become involved.

Nor did she wish to. Damaris held herself in check, giving no information about her experiences in the past, her feelings about the present, nor her thoughts and dreams about the future. Damaris was careful to reveal nothing about herself. [137]

Fear and shame cause us to hide who we are. Love and forgiveness cause us to show who God has made us.

And he [Adam] said, I heard thy voice in the garden, and I was afraid, because I *was* naked; and I hid myself.

GENESIS 3:10

PERFECT LOVE

Damaris could not believe what she was hearing. She had never seen a man "wash up" in her entire life.

"But—but I will do it," Damaris stammered.

"You may dry," conceded Miss Dover. "That is usually my chore—but this year—with the three of us—I'll care for the food and put the clean dishes away."

"But—but—I expected to do it all and I don't mind—really," Damaris hastily continued.

"Now, Miss Damaris," said Gil in his pleasant drawl, "if you wish to be a part of this little family, you must accept your assigned task without argument or conditions—or else pay the consequences. I learned that long ago." He smiled at Miss Dover, then turned to wink at Damaris, causing her cheeks to flame.

Damaris was too flustered to argue further. She hurriedly turned to the table and began to gather dinner plates and cutlery. The clean-up proceeded as planned, and Damaris listened to the light chatter and easy laughter. Gil had spoken of her as part of the family. In one way she longed to really be a part of what was going on around her. At the same time she held herself back. She dared not let her heart rule her head. [138–139]

When heart and head are not in agreement,
it is best to follow neither.

There is no fear in love; but perfect love casteth out fear: because fear hath torment. He that feareth is not made perfect in love.   1 JOHN 4:18

181

As Damaris listened to the chatter of her companions, she let her thoughts wander. Memories came rapidly—small scraps of disconnected pieces—yet they merged to make a disturbing whole. Christmases past had not been times of pleasure for Damaris. Nor would they be for her mama this Christmas, Damaris mused.

Any excuse for a celebration sent her pa scurrying off to the town saloon for as much whiskey as he could afford. Poor as he was, he always found money for too much liquor. Her mama would worry about his homecoming—hoping that it would be peaceful—and strangely—worry even more that he might not come home at all.

Damaris jerked her mind back to the present. She did not wish to think about home. It was much more pleasant here, in this room, with these two people. Gil made no mention of whiskey in connection with Christmas. Then she thought again of Captain Reilly and Mr. Brown. They hadn't used every excuse to find a bottle, either.

Maybe there really are men who don't drink, she concluded, wondering how many sober men she would have to know before she could finally believe one, finally trust one. [142]

> *We judge everything in light of our past experiences*
> *with others. God judges us in light of our*
> *past experience with Christ.*

My soul hath long dwelt with him that hateth peace. . . . The Lord shall preserve thee from all evil: he shall preserve thy soul.   PSALM 120:6; 121:7

GOD OUR FATHER

Miss Dover went to get her Bible from a nearby shelf. She passed it to Gil and he turned to the story of the first Christmas and the birth of the Christ Child. Damaris leaned forward to drink in the words. They seemed so—so powerful, so full of wonder. She longed to believe them, to accept them as truth.

When Gil finished, he laid aside the Bible and closed his eyes. Damaris continued to stare as he spoke words of recognition and thanksgiving for the love that prompted the events of long ago. Suddenly realizing that he was praying, Damaris ducked her head and shut her eyes tightly. Never before had she heard anyone pray. She felt as if she were walking across a newly scrubbed floor with dirty shoes. She squirmed, but even her discomfort could not keep her from straining to hear each word of the prayer.

Gil talked just as though he were speaking directly to God himself. Damaris had never heard anything like it in her entire life. You would have thought that Gil was best friends with the one to whom he was praying. And yet there was an earnestness, a hushed appreciation to his voice. Damaris could not understand it. [143]

Those who haven't been loved by their earthly father have a difficult time understanding the love of a heavenly Father.

For ye have not received the spirit of bondage again to fear; but ye have received the Spirit of adoption, whereby we cry, Abba, Father.   ROMANS 8:15

Damaris lifted her eyes and nodded her head. She could not find her voice, but she did manage to look up at him for just a minute. She saw understanding in the blue eyes before she quickly looked down again.

Confusion made her head whirl. A minute ago she had decided to stay out of his way. It had seemed so settled. And then he offered her a gift, a beautiful Christmas gift of lace for a new dress. If she accepted it, how could she then refuse to become a part of this—this strange yet beautiful family?

She wished he had not brought the gift for her. She wished she could hand it back. She wished Gil and Miss Dover were not standing there looking at her. Accepting her. Welcoming her. [145]

Being accepted is sometimes more frightening than not
being accepted, for when we become a part
of something else we allow others
to become a part of us.

He hath made us accepted in the beloved.

EPHESIANS 1:6

WOUNDS OF THE SPIRIT

What had gone on in the dining room? Damaris took a step toward her bedroom but just as she moved, the door to the kitchen opened and Mrs. Stacy stepped through. Her hair was disheveled, her eyes swollen, and her face dark with anger and frustration.

"Oh, there you are," she said as she jerked to a stop. "I was about to send someone over to get you. We've got a terrible mess in the dining room. That—that ol' fool of a miner—" Mrs. Stacy got no further. She flung her apron over her face and burst into tears.

Then the sheriff poked his head through the door. "Mrs. Stacy could use a cup of good strong tea," he said to Damaris. "Her place has been pretty much torn apart."

Damaris nodded. The kettle was still steaming, so she went for the teapot and the tea. "Here you are, Mrs. Stacy," said Damaris, passing the woman the cup of strong tea. Damaris wasn't sure if Mrs. Stacy heard; she was still crying loudly into her apron. Damaris could detect no cuts or bruises on the woman, but she knew that many painful injuries could be hidden. [148–149]

Wounds to the spirit can cause death
if we go to anyone but Christ for healing.

For I *am* poor and needy, and my heart is wounded within me.   PSALM 109:22

REVENGE

Without warning, anger started to burn within Damaris. It was the whiskey. No, it was those who were foolish enough and selfish enough to drink the vile stuff. Selfishness—that's what it was. No consideration for anyone else, for how they felt, or for how they suffered. Such people didn't deserve love. They didn't even deserve to live. It would serve them right if they fell in their stupor and bashed in their stupid heads. Mrs. Stacy was right. Let the no-good miner freeze to death in jail.

Never in all of her years of being the victim of her father's rages had Damaris felt such sudden and intense anger. It shocked her, but she did not repent. For a moment she even wished she had stayed at home and fought back. She was older now. Stronger. She was sure that she and her mama could put up quite a fight. They might not win, but they could inflict some damage before they were beaten. In that awful moment, Damaris longed for the chance to cause bruise for bruise, cut for cut, cruelty for cruelty.

And then, as quickly as it had come, the rage was gone, leaving Damaris trembling and troubled. Should she feel shame? Remorse? Damaris could not sort her troubled thoughts. She cleaned the mess as quickly as she could so she could retire to peace and quiet. [150]

To respond to injustice with revenge is foolish
because the result of revenge is never justice.

Dearly beloved, avenge not yourselves, but *rather* give place unto wrath: for it is written, Vengeance *is* mine; I will repay, saith the Lord. ROMANS 12:19

WHAT'S IN A NAME

Damaris was disappointed in the turn the story had taken. She read on and on, hoping it would return to the woman Damaris. But the more she read, the more it was apparent that the story of Damaris was sadly lacking. There was no more there. Nothing about the woman. The next chapters and verses went on to speak of others and what they had done.

Damaris concluded that she must have missed something. She flipped back to Acts 17:34 and read the verse again and again. Finally her mind accepted what her brain had been trying to tell her. There was nothing more said about Damaris. No words, no mighty exploits, no acts of kindness or deeds of bravery. She had done nothing. Said nothing.

With an angry thrust she pushed the Bible from her and heard it fall to the floor with a sickening thud. She did not even lean over to blow out her lamp. She pulled her blankets up about her ears, buried her face in her pillow, and let the tears flow.

Never had Damaris felt so completely defeated, so alone and miserable. Even the Bible had nothing to say about Damaris. She had been rejected by both heaven and earth. [152–153]

> *Just because we find our name in the Bible*
> *doesn't mean God will find our name in the Book of Life.*

Howbeit certain men clave unto him, and believed: among the which *was* Dionysius the Areopagite, and a woman named Damaris, and others with them.

ACTS 17:34

WORTH

Damaris felt a heaviness as she climbed from her bed and dressed for her duties of the day, and not all of it was due to her lack of sleep. She could not put into words the deep sorrow that settled over her after her discovery of the night before. There was nothing—nothing to the story of the Bible Damaris. No wonder Miss Dover had looked at her blankly when she mentioned that her name came from Scripture. Nobody, not even one as faithful at reading her Bible as Miss Dover, could possibly have paid any attention to the one-line account.

Damaris felt her cheeks grow warm with shame. How would she ever be able to face the kind woman again? The woman who knew her secret. Damaris had thought her biblical name gave her worth; now she knew that the woman in the Bible was of no account. Damaris left her room with a heavy heart and put her mind to the morning tasks.

Burying herself in her task had worked in the past, but it did not work well for Damaris on this difficult morning.   [155]

Having our name in God's Word doesn't give us worth,
but having God's Word in us makes us worthy.

Thy word have I hid in mine heart, that I might not sin against
thee.   PSALM 119:11

188

BELIEF IN CHRIST

Miss Dover looked up from her reading and beamed at Damaris as though she should be pleased. Damaris was more confused than ever. Those were exactly the same words she had read for herself.

"Don't you see?" asked the woman beside her.

Damaris shook her head. "She didn't do anything."

"But she did! She believed! Oh, Damaris, that is the most exciting, the most important thing anyone can ever do."

"Believed what?" asked Damaris.

"The message Paul brought to Athens about Jesus. About Him being the Son of God. The Savior. That we can be freed—forgiven—by trusting Him. You must go back. Read the chapter again and again until you understand it. Find out for yourself why it was so important that Damaris believed. I'll be praying for you as you read—that you might discover the truth for yourself."

Damaris nodded dumbly. She would go back and read—as many times as it took—until she could understand why Miss Dover was so excited about the fact that the Damaris of the Scriptures had believed the report of the man called Paul.   [160–161]

> *Belief in Christ is the point on which all of life revolves*
> *and without which life is pointless.*

> This Jesus, whom I preach unto you, is Christ. . . . That they
> should seek the Lord . . . for in him we live, and move, and
> have our being.   ACTS 17:3, 28

COMFORT

It took Damaris many days and many readings until she began to understand the meaning of the Scriptures, but at last she was able to put the stories of the life and death of Christ together with the persistent teaching of the Apostle Paul. "It is true," she whispered to herself as she lay tucked in her bed one night. "All the stories about Him are true. He really lived—and died—and lives again. And I can know Him. Can know Him—in my—my very being. In my heart. My mind. I don't really know the spot—but I know that He can be with me—in me—just as the Bible says."

That night, tucked under blankets to ward off the chill of the room, Damaris became a believer. Warmth more comforting than that of any quilt flooded her whole being as she took the important step of faith. She still had much to learn. She still had many troublesome scars from her past that needed healing, but she knew one thing with certainty. She was a believer. Just like the Damaris of the Bible.

She was so anxious to share her discovery with Miss Dover that she found it difficult to sleep. She knew that the older woman would be thrilled to know that her prayers had been answered.   [161]

Earthly comfort becomes less important to us
when the heavenly comforter dwells within us.

The Comforter, *which is* the Holy Ghost . . . shall teach you all things, and bring all things to your remembrance, whatsoever I have said unto you.

JOHN 14:26

HIDING BITTERNESS

Damaris lived with the joy and peace of her newfound faith for two years before her past began to trouble her. Gradually she became aware of her intense feelings toward her father. She had tried to push aside the anger that accompanied her thoughts about him. He was just some distressing presence from her past. She was through with him—finished. Why should he bother her now?

Yet as Damaris continued to read the Bible with greater understanding, she kept coming across disturbing passages that spoke of forgiveness—of love. She began to wonder if the Jesus she now served expected her to forgive one who had so often and so cruelly wronged her.

Try as she might, Damaris could not push aside the matter as easily as she once had. But neither could she forgive. She struggled with her problem but she did not discuss it. Not even with Miss Dover. Damaris pretended there was no bitterness buried within her—and for the most part, she succeeded in hiding it from others.

[163]

Trying to hide bitterness is like heating the contents of a tightly sealed jar. An explosion is inevitable if the pressure isn't released.

Forbearing one another, and forgiving one another, if any man have a quarrel against any: even as Christ forgave you, so also *do* ye.   COLOSSIANS 3:13

PUTTING AWAY ANGER

Damaris had her own Bible now. Miss Dover had seen to that. Damaris had never had such a treasured possession, and she read it before going to the kitchen in the morning and before retiring at night. She memorized verses that caught her attention and reviewed them silently as she worked on one task or another. Every day she learned and grew—but she did not release her bitterness. She simply tried to smother it with the positive lessons she was learning daily.

There were many days when things went well and Damaris could forget that she had ever felt angry, bitter, and alone. She had her God. She could talk to Him as a friend—just as Gil had done that first Christmas she had spent at Miss Dover's. She had her Bible. She could turn to its pages for strength and direction. She even had friends—Gil would say "family," but Damaris still found it difficult to consider herself part of the family. [164]

*Anger that we can keep taking out
has not been properly put away.*

And grieve not the holy Spirit of God, whereby ye are sealed unto the day of redemption. Let all bitterness, and wrath, and anger, and clamour, and evil speaking, be put away from you, with all malice.

EPHESIANS 4:30–31

SIN IS SIN

Damaris placed the flour and yeast in a small brown bag and was passing it to the woman when a man burst through the door, slamming it back against the wall and making everything shudder. He strode to the counter, jerked the brown bag away from the woman, and threw it at Damaris. "I suppose this is your doin'," he growled. "Talkin' her into spendin' my money on yer foolish notions."

The woman cowered as though expecting to be struck. The little girl dodged behind her mother's skirts, and the little boy ducked behind a wooden barrel. But Abbie stood firm in her place, prepared to take the brunt of the assault.

The smell of whiskey was all too familiar to Damaris. Anger rose up within her and gave her boldness. She pushed herself to her full height, ready to give the man a piece of her mind, but the terrified look in the woman's eyes stopped her short. Challenging him would only bring more pain to the family. Damaris turned aside, defeated again. She knew then that her old hatred had not been removed, only buried deeper within her. [170–171]

Allowing hatred to consume us
is as bad as consuming too much alcohol.

Now the works of the flesh are manifest, which are . . . hatred . . . drunkenness . . . of the which I tell you . . . that they which do such things shall not inherit the kingdom of God.　　GALATIANS 5:19–21

THE SIN OF PARENTS

Damaris thought of the little girl with the big blue-green eyes.

"It's a shame about the father——" began Gil.

"No!" said Damaris quickly. "No, it isn't. It's——"

"You know him?" asked Gil.

"I've seen him a few times," she said slowly.

"And you didn't care much for what you saw?" questioned Gil.

"No," said Damaris. "I did not care for what I saw."

"And what did you see?" Gil probed.

"I——I called on the home when Miss Dover and I started our Sunday school. He——he was very angry. Said his children didn't need any——any part of it. He——he had been drinking. I could smell it. Then Mrs. Rudding came to the store one day. Wanted a few groceries. Just flour——and yeast. She had the coins, but he tore the bag away from her and accused me of causing her to spend his money foolishly. He had been drinking then too."

Damaris shivered. She pulled her shawl more closely about herself, pretending that the tremor came from the cold weather rather than from her frightening childhood memories. [175–176]

Our children inherit not only what we have spent
our money on but also what we have spent
our energy on——whether good or bad.

The iniquity of the fathers [is visited] upon the children, and upon the children's children, unto the third and to the fourth *generation.*　　　　EXODUS 34:7

PROTECTION

How could she explain to Gil her past and its effect on her? She didn't even understand it herself, and she could never talk about it to anyone else. No one would understand the fear, the torture of suspense, the anger that burned deep within, the stripping of self-worth, the feeling of being totally at the mercy of another.

"If you won't take my coat, sit closer," insisted Gil. "Let me shield you from the wind."

Damaris felt her cheeks glow with embarrassment as Gil turned her slightly so that she would be protected from the wind by his larger frame. She wanted to escape, but she held herself rigidly in place and soon had to acknowledge that he was right. It was much warmer up closer to him where the wind no longer could flutter her light shawl.

[176]

In the plan of God,
the healthy will care for the sick,
the rich will feed the poor, and
the strong will protect the weak.

And a man shall be as an hiding place from the wind, and a covert from the tempest; as rivers of water in a dry place, as the shadow of a great rock in a weary land.

ISAIAH 32:2

A HEAVY HEART

Mrs. Rudding clung to life, but tenuously. Then a message came by wire from a neighboring town to the sheriff. A man bearing the description of Sam Rudding had been killed in a brawl a couple weeks earlier. It seemed that the children were without a father.

Damaris felt no regret when she learned of the man's death, but then her conscience began to upbraid her.

He is lost and doomed to hell, a voice said.

And I can't think of anyone who deserves it more, her own bitter voice answered.

Is that a Christian attitude? Would Jesus have responded in such a manner? asked the first voice.

Damaris did not answer. Though she knew what the answer would be. That night when she knelt to pray, her soul was heavy. "God, I need help," she whispered. "I can't carry this load anymore. Bitterness weighs down my soul. It will destroy me if—if something isn't done. But I can't let go. I can't. I've tried. I can't let go."

Damaris cried into her pillow again, but her heavy burden was not made lighter. [184]

The only way to lighten a heavy heart
is to fill it up with love.

Heaviness in the heart of man maketh it stoop: but a good word maketh it glad.

PROVERBS 12:25

THE PURPOSE OF LIFE

Gil brought the sad news. Mrs. Rudding had passed away.

"What's going to happen to the children?" Damaris asked quietly.

Gil shifted his weight, his face drawn. "They are to have a hearing sometime next week to decide," he answered.

"Poor little souls," said Miss Dover.

Damaris excused herself from the room. She needed to get out. To think. Something had to be done but she had no notion of what it was. Into her mind came the face of the children: Abbie, eyes big with pain and grief; William, skinny and under-sized for lack of nourishing food; and little Tootles, still confused and whining for her mama. Life seemed so unfair. Damaris might have gone under with the cruelness of it all had she not had two years of walking and talking with her Lord. Even now, she was deeply troubled. "What's the meaning of it all, God?" she asked, lifting her face to the sky. "Why is the world so heartless? So painful?" [185]

When we question the purpose of life
we can have confidence in the purpose of God.

For this purpose the Son of God was manifested, that he might destroy the works of the devil.

1 JOHN 3:8

TEARS TRANSFORMED

When Damaris spoke she surprised herself with her daring question. "Miss Dover said you grew up in an orphanage. What was it like?"

Gil's eyes darkened for a moment; then he turned to her and answered candidly, "Not nice. We each had our own little bed, our own shelf area for our one change of clothes, our own dish at the table, our own second-hand pair of shoes." He paused. "But that wasn't the hard part," he went on. "The hard part was not having anyone on your side. All of the kids stood alone, like we were afraid to stick together. Each individual against the entire force of—of disciplinarians." He paused longer this time.

Damaris looked at him and saw the pain in his eyes and the working of his jaw. He picked up a small stone and tossed it at an old tin pot lying half-buried several feet away. Then he went on. "They called it a 'home.' But it wasn't. Not in any sense. The rules were rigid. The discipline tough. We were not even allowed to cry."

[186–187]

God does not stifle our tears;
He turns them into joy.

They that sow in tears shall reap in joy.

PSALM 126:5

GOD'S WORK IN US

They sat quietly for a few more minutes and then Damaris broke the silence.

"Are you bitter?"

Gil's head came up and he looked directly into the deep brown eyes. "Bitter? Why?" he asked frankly.

"Well—about life? About your circumstances? I mean—you had nothing to do with your folks dying. Just like I had nothing to do with my pa drinking."

Gil spoke softly. "Guess I was. Once. Before I met Miss Dover. Then after—after she finally broke through the barrier I had put up, and taught me from her Bible, well, after I had accepted God's Word as truth and asked for forgiveness for my own wrongdoing, then I was slowly able to forgive others too."

"I can't," admitted Damaris. "I still can't. I've tried—but I just can't."

"I don't suppose we ever can—on our own. Only God can work that miracle." [188]

We do not have the ability to want what is good
any more than we have the ability to do it apart from God.

For it is God which worketh in you both to will and to do of *his* good pleasure.

PHILIPPIANS 2:13

200

PURPOSE OF PAIN

I suppose each person has to work it out in his own way," said Gil slowly. "For me—it was—well, the realization that all things happen for good. Oh, not the orphanage really, or the drink, either. That wasn't part of God's plan. But even the bad in life has a purpose, I think."

"A purpose? What good can possibly come from—from so—so much bad?"

"I'm not sure how to—how to say it. But thinking of it like that—it helped me get over my hurt. I—well, I said to myself— that if I accepted my past—put it to use in my life—then it wouldn't be wasted. I mean—it seems to me that painful experiences can be used to better prepare us for heaven. You see, if we let it, even pain can shape us—make us better people—get rid of some of the ugly parts of our humanity."

"It only strengthened my ugliness," confessed Damaris.

"But it doesn't need to," insisted Gil. "It can make us stronger, more compassionate, more understanding—more like Jesus—if we allow it to. And the more clutter we get rid of in our life here—the more we will be able to enjoy heaven—when we get there. So, pain can have a purpose." [188–189]

If we've been transformed by Christ,
we cannot be deformed by pain.

And we know that all things work together for good to them
that love God, to them who are the called according to *his*
purpose.   ROMANS 8:28

FIT FOR HEAVEN

Well, I know I don't explain it well—but—say—say two people are going on a journey. One prepares. He buys the right clothing for the climate. He reads all he can to learn about the area. He studies about the people. Learns the language. He gets himself prepared the best he can. The other fella—he just goes. They both get there—to the same place. But which one do you think will enjoy it the most?"

"I s'pose the one who prepared," admitted Damaris.

"Exactly. I think that is why—why God allows hard things in life. To prepare us. To knock off rough edges—pride, bias, envy, selfishness—so that when we get to heaven we will be more in tune—more able to enjoy the beautiful things we'll find there. Maybe that's what the rewards will be. A deeper appreciation of what we are given—what we are a part of. Do you understand what I am muddling through?"

Damaris nodded her head slowly. "I—I think so," she answered.

"Well, I don't know if it makes any sense to anyone else—but for me—well, it gives a special purpose—a meaning for suffering. If we take it right—let it shape us and cleanse us—then we are better prepared to enjoy the glories of heaven." [189]

To be fit for heaven we must exercise on earth.

Exercise thyself . . . unto godliness. For bodily exercise profiteth little: but godliness is profitable unto all things, having promise of the life that now is, and of that which is to come.   1 TIMOTHY 4:7–8

LOVE CONQUERS HATE

Damaris did not spend long in her prayer time. It did not take long. She was weary of her heavy burden of bitterness. She wanted to make the pain and disappointments of the past into stepping-stones for growth. "Take my bitterness, Lord," she prayed. "Please, take it from me. Cleanse my heart and help me to forgive. Might I be able to use my experience to be more understanding, more compassionate, more loving. Might it make me a better person so that I might appreciate heaven more when I arrive. Make me more like you, Lord Jesus."

After a time of earnest prayer, the terrible burden lifted.

"Mama—I love you," Damaris whispered softly, even though she was all alone. "I—I wish that I would have told you so. I hope you know."

Then Damaris had a new thought, and her heart swelled with the knowledge of it. Her Mama loved her. Yet her mother had never spoken of it either.

"That's why you urged me to go. You loved me. You didn't want me to be the victim anymore. You decided to take it all—yourself."

[190]

When we allow God to haul away our hatred we can finally see the love that's been buried beneath it.

He that loveth not knoweth not God; for God is love. . . . And we have known and believed the love that God hath to us. God is love; and he that dwelleth in love dwelleth in God, and God in him.   1 JOHN 4:8, 16

OUTWARD APPEARANCE

Damaris leaned her head into her hands and cried. "If—if only Pa didn't—" she began, then stopped abruptly. "I—I guess he was a victim too," she said aloud. "I had never thought of that. Never wondered what made him who he is. Never even thought to ask what kind of home he grew up in. I wonder if—if his pa beat him. I wonder when drink got such a hold on him."

Damaris ran a shaky hand through her hair and prayed, "Oh, God, help me to love Pa. Help me to somehow forgive the terrible things he's done. Help me to pray for him—like I pray for Mama."

After a few moments Damaris wiped her eyes on the hem of her dress. Then she rose and brushed her skirts. "I'm a mess," she observed, one hand stealing to her hastily pinned hair as her eyes surveyed her wrinkled dress—and then she smiled. "But I'm in better shape on the inside than I have ever been." [190–191]

Folks who try too hard to look good on the outside
might be trying to cover what's on the inside.

Create in me a clean heart, O God; and renew a right spirit
within me.   PSALM 51:10

FALLING IN LOVE

Gil was on his way in with William hoisted up on his neck. The boy's hands were buried in the depths of Gil's brown curly hair, and Gil's Stetson was falling down over William's eyes. Even from the distance, Damaris could see the pleased look on the little boy's face. Abbie was bouncing along ahead of Gil, talking excitedly and waving a hand now and then at the corral and its cattle.

The revelation came to Damaris without warning. She lifted a hand to her breast and a little gasp caught in her throat. At that very moment she realized with startling clarity that she loved Gil Lewis. She closed her eyes tightly and put out a hand to stop the room from swirling around her.

She loved him! Her fear of him had long ago changed to comfort, then to respect, then sharing, and a measure of dependency. But when had her feelings turned to love? She had no business loving him. What would she ever do now? Her first thought was to flee. But that was impossible. *He'll know*, she said to herself. *He'll see it in my face and I'll be so embarrassed.* Then she reprimanded herself. "Be calm," she said firmly. "You've hidden your feelings before. Surely you can do it again."

[214–215]

Failing to love is reason to be ashamed,
but falling in love is not.

And now abideth faith, hope, charity, these three; but the greatest of these *is* charity.

1 CORINTHIANS 13:13

SURRENDER

Dusk was settling, but Damaris could still see plainly as she opened the door a crack. Gil stood there, an apologetic smile on his lips, his worn Stetson in his hands.

Damaris opened the door quickly, her thoughts leaping to Miss Dover. "There's nothing wrong, is there?" she asked anxiously.

"Yes," he admitted, his head cocked slightly to one side, his eyes burning into hers. "There is! I can't eat. I can't sleep. I can't even do my work." He brushed past her into the house, tossed his hat onto a nearby chair, and turned to face her. "I love you, Damaris. I want you to be my wife. I know I don't have much to offer you, but I promise—you will have everything I do have. My love. My devotion. My respect. I—"

Damaris flung herself into his arms. Her own arms encircled his neck and she leaned against his tall frame and cried against his shoulder. She had heard the words she had longed to hear. He loved her.   [218]

Surrendering to each other
is the only way to win in love.

For this cause shall a man leave his father and mother, and
shall be joined unto his wife, and they two shall be one flesh.

EPHESIANS 5:31